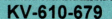

A Whimsey Anthology

Collected by

Carolyn Wells

New York

Charles Scribner's Sons

1906

A WHIMSEY ANTHOLOGY

" . . . where care
None is, slight things do lightly please."

ROBERT HERRICK.

PREFACE

A WHIMSEY is defined by the dictionaries as a whim, a freak, a capricious notion, an odd device. Though of trifling value as literary efforts, verbal whimseys often display such ingenuity and patience of labor that they command, perforce, a certain admiration.

Many of the best and most learned of writers have amused themselves in making these oddities, but as modern times offer little leisure for such work, the best examples are oftenest found among the works of the earlier authors.

A literary whimsey is not merely the expression of a whimsical thought or fancy, but an odd or capricious form of that expression. It is whimseys of manner not matter that are offered in this collection.

CONTENTS

LOGICAL WHIMSEYS

[vii]

Contents

[viii]

Contents

[ix]

Contents

[x]

Contents

Contents

BLANK VERSE IN PROSE

FIXED FORMS

CHAIN VERSE

Contents

[xiii]

Contents

PUNNING WHIMSEYS

TRAVESTIES OR WHIMSICAL BURLESQUES

Contents

[xv]

Contents

SEY ANTHOLOGY

A WHIMSEY ANTHOLOGY

A Whimsey Anthology

LOGICAL WHIMSEYS*

CONJUGAL CONJUGATIONS

DEAR maid, let me speak
What I never yet spoke:
You have made my heart squeak
As it never yet squoke,
And for sight of you, both my eyes ache as they
ne'er before oak.

With your voice my ears ring,
And a sweeter ne'er rung,
Like a bird's on the wing
When at morn it has wung.
And gladness to me it doth bring, such as never
voice brung.

My feelings I'd write,
But they cannot be wrote,
And who can indite
What was never indote!
And my love I hasten to plight—the first that I
plote.

* Logical effects of grammar, spelling, pronunciation, etc.

[3]

Yes, you would I choose,
    Whom I long ago chose,
And my fond spirit sues
    As it never yet sose,
And ever on you do I muse, as never man mose.

The house where you bide
    Is a blessed abode;
Sure, my hopes I can't hide,
    For they will not be hode,
And no person living has sighed, as, darling, I've
    sode.

Your glances they shine
    As no others have shone,
And all else I'd resign
    That a man could resone,
And surely no other could pine as I lately have pone.

And don't you forget
    You will ne'er be forgot,
You never should fret
    As at times you have frot,
I would chase all the cares that beset, if they ever
    besot.

For you I would weave
    Songs that never were wove,
And deeds I'd achieve
    Which no man yet achove,
And for me you never should grieve, as for you I
    have grove.

[4]

I'm as worthy a catch
As ever was caught.
O, your answer I watch
As a man never waught,
And we'd make the most elegant match as ever was
maught.

Let my longings not sink;
I would die if they sunk.
O, I ask you to think
As you never have thunk,
And our fortunes and lives let us link, as no lives
could be lunk.

A. W. Bellaw.

LOVE'S MOODS AND SENSES

SALLY SALTER, she was a young lady who
taught,
And her friend Charley Church was a preacher who praught!
Though his enemies called him a screecher who
scraught.

His heart when he saw her kept sinking and sunk,
And his eye, meeting hers, began winking and wunk;
While she in her turn fell to thinking, and thunk.

He hastened to woo her, and sweetly he wooed,
For his love grew until to a mountain it grewed,
And what he was longing to do then he doed.

[5]

In secret he wanted to speak, and he spoke,
To seek with his lips what his heart long had soke;
So he managed to let the truth leak, and it loke.

He asked her to ride to the church, and they rode,
They so sweetly did glide, that they both thought
        they glode,
And they came to the place to be tied, and were
        tode.

Then, "homeward" he said, "let us drive" and
        they drove,
And soon as they wished to arrive, they arrove;
For whatever he couldn't contrive she controve.

The kiss he was dying to steal, then he stole:
At the feet where he wanted to kneel, then he knole,
And said, "I feel better than ever I fole."

So they to each other kept clinging, and clung;
While time his swift circuit was winging, and wung;
And this was the thing he was bringing, and brung:

The man Sally wanted to catch, and had caught—
That she wanted from others to snatch, and had
        snaught—
Was the one that she now liked to scratch, and
        she scraught.

And Charley's warm love began freezing and froze,
While he took to teasing, and cruelly toze
The girl he had wished to be squeezing and squoze.

[6]

"Wretch!" he cried, when she threatened to leave
    him, and left,
"How could you deceive me, as you have deceft?"
And she answered, "I promised to cleave, and
    I've cleft!"

Anonymous.

AN ORIGINAL LOVE STORY

H E struggled to kiss her. She struggled the
    same
        To prevent him so bold and undaunted.
But, as smitten by lightning, he heard her exclaim,
    "Avaunt, sir!" and off he avaunted.

But when he returned, with a wild fiendish laugh,
    Showing clearly that he was affronted,
And threaten'd by main force to carry her off,
    She cried "Don't!" and the poor fellow donted.

When he meekly approached, and sat down at her
    feet,
    Praying loudly, as before he had ranted,
That she would forgive him, and try to be sweet,
    And said "Can't you!" the dear girl recanted.

Then softly he whispered, "How could you do so?
    I certainly thought I was jilted;
But come thou with me, to the parson we'll go;
    Say, wilt thou, my dear?" and she wilted.

Anonymous.

[7]

"QUERIES"

A BRED and born philologist is what I claim
　　　to be,
　　　But find that there are many things that
　　　　greatly puzzle me.
For instance, take a cricket ball; you buy it—then
　　it's bought,
But if you take and shy it, is it right to say it's
　　short?
A drummer is a man, we know, who has to do
　　with drums,
But I never met a plumber yet who had to do with
　　plums.
A cheerful man who sells you hats would be a
　　cheerful hatter;
But is a serious man who sells you mats "a serious
　　matter"?

You take your girl to Yarmouth, then you are a
　　pair of trippers;
If you slipped with her while skating, would you
　　be a pair of slippers?
If it freezes when it's frosty, is it squosty when
　　you squeeze?
Would you have to buy a biograph to write biog-
　　raphies?
A man is called a baker when to earn his bread
　　he bakes;
But do we call a Quaker by that name because
　　he quakes?

[8]

But if you are a dealer, why, of course you have
    to deal,
But you may be a peeler, though you never have
    to peel.

A man who brews, as everybody knows, is called
    a brewer;
But if your landlord sues you, would you say he
    is a sewer?
A girl will change the color of the hair upon her
    head;
It's strange; but, still, you'll find that though she
    dyed, she isn't dead.
Would a pious man who fried a kipper be a holy
    friar?
A timid man who lies in bed—is he "a fearful
    liar"?
If with mud you find you're spattered from a pass-
    ing horse's hoof,
And you use a bad expletive, would that be a
    "muddied oaf"?

W. Stanford.

THE BALLAD OF AMEIGHLIA MAIREIGH.

MISS Amelia Mary Cholmondely,
    When in summer-time she rode,
    Did not look one whit less colmondley
    Than in winter when she slode.

[9]

As became a farmer's daughter,
  Milk she to the market took;
Mingled flour and eggs with waughter,
  And delicious tea-cakes book.

By her blandishments the neighing
  Colts and bleating sheep were caught;
And, they tell me, there's no seighing
  What a lot of ricks she thaught.

At her orders farm-yard beauties—
  Turkeys, geese, and hens—were slain;
From her purse, for weekly deauties,
  All her father's men were pain.

Mary, too, was always present
  When the frisky lambs were shorn;
And the chicks of many a phesent
  By her careful hands were rorn.

'Spite of Mary's fond endeavour,
  Once her favorite lap-dog swam
Far from land and sank foreavour,
  And her eyes with sorrow dam.

Girl more kind or better-hearted
  Ne'er in all my life I saw;
Scores of swains for Mary smearted,
  She was perfect, all agraw.

Thus, when to Elisha Farquhar
    Hand and heart at last she gave,
Though he was a billiard-marqahar,
    Happily with him she lave.

Anonymous.

THE PEARL OF PALENCIA

NO maiden in Spain was more lovely to see
    Than sweet Donna A., only child of Don B.,
    "The Pearl of Palencia." Two lovers she had,
Don C. (who was good) and Don D. (who was bad).
'Twas C. she preferr'd, but she thought herself bound
To mind her papa, whom she always had mound.
He said, "Rich Don D. is a 'catch' to be caught:
The prize you must snatch—it is easily snaught."
Thus, though she might feel just the same as she'd felt,
She now must conceal what she'd never con celt;
Not speak to her love, though he tenderly spoke,
Nor seek the affection she'd hitherto soke.
Don B. told Don C. he must leave, and he left.
The blow made him grieve, and most deeply he greft;
But Love's sun will shine, and still brightly it shone.
When lovers combine—as these lovers combone,

[11]

In secret to meet—as they secretly met,
Stern parents they'll cheat—as her father was chet.
One night when the moon on "the rise" gently
    rose,
Don D. in surprise the two lovers surprose.
His weapon he drew; and the moment 'twas
    drawn,
His rival he slew; with a blow he was slawn.
Prepared not to smite, and so suddenly smitten,
He'd no time to fight, or of course he'd have fitten,
His fate was to fall—what a cropper he fell!
A sight to appal. Donna A. it appel.
Her hand, within reach, with an effort he reach'd,
And this was the "last dying speech" that he
    speech'd:
"Dear maid, fare thee well! Be my slayer for-
    given;
My hour, but too quick to arrive, hath arriven.
Away from existence I slide"—and he slid.
"I die as my fathers have died"—and he did.
Oh, fearful to hear was the scream that she
    scrempt!
Her eyes did not beam as they'd hitherto bempt,
But glared fit to freeze. The assassin they froze.
She shrieked, "This I seize!"—'twas a dagger
    she soze.
"My loved one I lose—through thy deed he is
    lost;
But had I to choose, thou wouldst never be
    chost.
Die, villain! Thy gold cannot gild up thy guilt.
My will is to kill!" So the villain she kilt.

Then said, "Though my heart, doomed to break,
   is now broken,
The vengeance I thirsted to slake I have sloken."
So saying, she drank up a poisonous draught,
Her queenly form shrank with a terrible shraft;
On C.'s poor remains with a wild fling 'twas
   flung;
Her spirit, which long'd to take wing, then took
   wung.
Her pa—"such a turn" the catastrophe gave—
Did grieve till he grove himself into his grave.
So there was an end—lack-a-day! woe is me!—
Of sweet Donna A. and Dons B., C., and D.
                    Walter Parke.

OUGH

A S a farmer was going to plough,
   He met a man driving a cough;
   They had words which led to a rough,
And the farmer was struck on his brough.

One day when the weather was rough,
An old lady went for some snough,
Which she thoughtlessly placed in her mough,
And it got scattered all over her cough.

While a baker was kneading his dough,
A weight fell down on his tough,
When he suddenly exclaimed ough!
Because it had hurt him sough.

[13]

There was a hole in the hedge to get through,
It was made by no one knew whough;
In getting through a boy lost his shough,
And was quite at a loss what to dough.

A poor old man had a bad cough,
To a doctor he straight went ough,
The doctor did nothing but scough,
And said it was all fancy, his cough.

Anonymous.

O-U-G-H *

A Fresh Hack at an Old Knot

I'M taught P-l-o-u-g-h
    S'all be pronounce "plow."
   "Zat's easy w'en you know," I say,
    "Mon Anglais, I'll get through!"

My teacher say zat in zat case,
    O-u-g-h is "oo."
An zen I laugh and say to him,
    "Zees Anglais make me cough."

He say "Not 'coo,' but in zat word,
    O-u-g-h is 'off,'"
Oh, *Sacre bleu*! such varied sounds
    Of words makes my hiccough!

* By permission of Harper & Brothers.

He say, "Again mon frien' ees wrong;
  O-u-g-h is 'up'
In hiccough." Zen I cry, "No more,
  You make my t'roat feel rough."

"Non, non!" he cry, "you are not right;
  O-u-g-h is 'uff.'"
I say, "I try to spik your words,
  I cannot spik zem though!"

"In time you'll learn, but now you're wrong!
  O-u-g-h is 'owe.'"
"I'll try no more, I s'all go mad,
  I'll drown me in ze lough!"

"But ere you drown yourself," said he,
  "O-u-g-h is 'ock'"
He taught no more, I held him fast,
  And killed him wiz a rough.
Charles Battell Loomis.

OW

NOW, boys," the farmer said, "there'll be a
    row
  If you upon the river go and row
When we've so much to do. The Chester sow
  Has rooted up the lawn; therein go sow
Some clover-seed; then help clear out the mow.
  In which to put the hay that we shall mow

[15]

To-morrow morn; when that is done I 'low
  You may, if then the sun is not too low,
Go hunt and fish." So to our work we bow;
  Which done, we're off, with arrows, rod, and
    bow.

Anonymous.

ADIOUX AMONG THE SIOUX

NOW trouble brious among the Sioux,
  Because the whites their rights abioux.
  The sky is red with battle hioux;
Big Injun, squaw, and young pappioux
Are on the war-path by the slioux;
They're filling up with fiery bioux,
They swear their lands they will not lioux.

Anonymous.

JOB

OUR hired man named Job
  Has got a pleasant job,
  The meadow grass to mow
  And stow it in the mow.

At work he takes the lead;
He does not fear cold lead,
Nor is he moved to tears
When he his clothing tears!

[16]

A book that he had read;
He handed me to read;
He spends much time in reading
When at his home in Reading.

Anonymous.

THE COW—A BOVINITY

O gentle cau,
  Contented frau,
    Inert, exempt from violence.
We will allau
  That you know hau
To chew your cud in siolence.

Anonymous.

HALF HOURS WITH THE CLASSICS

AH, those hours when by-gone sages
    Led our thoughts through Learning's ways,
When the wit of sunnier ages,
    Called once more to Earth the days
When rang through Athens' vine-hung lanes
Thy wild, wild laugh, Aristophanes!

Pensive through the land of Lotus,
  Sauntered we by Nilus' side;
Garrulous old Herodotus
  Still our mentor, still our guide,
Prating of the mystic bliss
Of Isis and of Osiris.

[17]

All the learn'd ones trooped before us,
　All the wise of Hellas' land,
Down from mythic Pythagoras,
　To the hemlock drinker grand.
Dark the hour that closed the gates
Of gloomy Dis on thee, Socrates.

Ah, those hours of tend'rest study,
　When Electra's poet told
Of Love's cheek once warm and ruddy,
　Pale with grief, with death chill cold!
Sobbing low like summer tides
Flow thy verses, Euripides!

High our hearts beat when Cicero
　Shook the Capitolian dome;
How we shuddered, watching Nero
　'Mid the glare of blazing Rome!
How those records still affright us
On thy gloomy page, Tacitus!

Back to youth I seem to glide, as
　I recall those by-gone scenes,
When we conned o'er Thucydides,
　Or recited Demosthenes.

L'ENVOI

Ancient sages, pardon these
Somewhat doubtful quantities.
　　　　　　　　H. J. DeBurgh.

SHAKE, MULLEARY AND GO-ETHE

I

I HAVE a bookcase, which is what
   Many much better men have not.
   There are no books inside, for books,
I am afraid, might spoil its looks.
But I've three busts, all second-hand,
Upon the top. You understand
I could not put them underneath—
Shake, Mulleary and Go-ethe.

II

Shake was a dramatist of note;
He lived by writing things to quote,
He long ago put on his shroud:
Some of his works are rather loud.
His bald-spot's dusty, I suppose.
I know there's dust upon his nose.
I'll have to give each nose a sheath—
Shake, Mulleary and Go-ethe.

III

Mulleary's line was quite the same;
He has more hair, but far less fame.

I would not from that fame retrench—
But he is foreign, being French.
Yet high his haughty head he heaves,
The only one done up in leaves,
They're rather limited on wreath—
Shake, Mulleary and Go-ethe.

IV

Go-ethe wrote in the German tongue:
He must have learned it very young.
His nose is quite a butt for scoff,
Although an inch of it is off.
He did quite nicely for the Dutch;
But here he doesn't count for much.
They all are off their native heath—
Shake, Mulleary and Go-ethe.

V

They sit there, on their chests, as bland
As if they were not second-hand.
I do not know of what they think,
Nor why they never frown or wink.
But why from smiling they refrain
I think I clearly can explain:
They none of them could show much teeth—
Shake, Mulleary and Go-ethe.

H. C. Bunner.

SHAPED WHIMSEYS

_____

THE WINE GLASS

Who hath woe? Who hath sorrow? Who
hath contentions? Who hath wounds
without cause? Who hath redness
of eyes? They that tarry long
at the wine! They that
go to seek mixed wine!
Look not thou upon the
wine when it is red,
when it giveth
its color
in the
cup,
when it
moveth itself
aright.
At
the last it
biteth like a serpent
and stingeth like an adder!

(Proverbs xxiii, 29-32.)

SONG OF THE DECANTER

There was an old decan-
ter, and its mouth was
gaping wide; the
rosy wine had
ebbed away
and left
its crys-
tal side:
and the wind
went humming—
humming
up and
down: the
wind it blew,
and through the
reed-like
hollow neck
the wildest notes it
blew. I placed it in the
window, where the blast was
blowing free, and fancied that its
pale mouth sang the queerest strains to
me. "They tell me—puny conquerors! the
Plague has slain his ten, and war his hundred
thousand of the very best of men; but I"—'twas
thus the Bottle spake—"but I have conquered
more than all your famous conquerors, so
feared and famed of yore. Then come, ye
youths and maidens all, come drink from
out my cup, the beverage that dulls the
brain and burns the spirits up; that puts
to shame your conquerors that slay their
scores below; for this has deluged mil-
lions with the lava tide of woe. Tho'
in the path of battle darkest streams
of blood may roll; yet while I killed
the body, I have damn'd the very
soul. The cholera, the plague,
the sword, such ruin never wro't,
as I in mirth or malice on the
innocent have brought. And
still I breathe upon them, and
they shrink before my breath,
and year by year my thousands
tread the dusty way of death."

Anonymous.

[22]

THE FLAGON

Que mon
f l a c o n
me semble bon!
S a n s l u i
l ' e n n u i
me nuit,
me suit;
j e s e n s
m e s s e n s
mourants,
p e s a n t s.
Quand je le tiens,
Dieux! que je suis bien!
que son aspect est agréable!
que je fais cas de ses divins présens!
C'est de son sein fécond, c'est de ses heureux
flancs que coule ce nectar si doux, si délectable,
qui rend tous les esprits, tous les cœurs satisfaits!
Cher objet de mes vœux, tu fais toute ma gloire.
Tant que mon cœur vivra, de tes charmants bien-
faits il, saura conserver la fidèle mémoire.

Pannard.

THE GLASS

Nous ne pouvons rien trouver sur la terre
qui soit si bon ni si beau que le verre.
Du tendre amour berceau charmant,
c'est toi, champêtre fougère,
c'est toi qui sers à faire
l'heureux instrument
où souvent pétille,
mousse, et brille
le jus qui rend
gai, riant,
content.
Quelle douceur
il porte au cœur
tôt
tôt
tôt
Qu'on m'en donne
vite et comme il faut
tôt
tôt
tôt
qu'on m'en donne
vite et comme il faut.
L'on y voit sur ses flots
chéris nager l'allégresse et les ris.

Pannard.

[24]

BAIT OF THE AVERAGE FISHERMAN

This is the bait
the fisher-
men take,
the fishermen take, the fishermen take, when they start out the fish to
wake, so early in the morning. They take a nip before they go — a good one, ah! and long and slow,
for fear the chills will lay them low, so early in
the morning. Another — when they're on the
street, which they repeat each time they meet
for "luck" — for that's the way to greet a
fisher in the morning. And when they are
on the river's brink again they drink without a wink — to fight malaria they think
it proper in the morning. They tip a
flask with true delight when there's a
bite; if fishing's light they "smile"
the more, till jolly tight all fishing
they are scorning. Another nip as
they depart; one at the mart and
one to part; but none when in
the house they dart expecting
there'll be mourning. This
is the bait the fishermen try,
who fishes buy at prices
high, and tell each one
a bigger lie of fishing
in the morning.

H. C. Dodge.

[25]

A TYPE OF BEAUTY

Here
hang my bangs
o'er eyes that dream,
And nose and rose-
bud lips for cream.
And here's my
chin with dim-
ples in.
This is my
neck with-
out a speck,
which doth these snowy shoulders
deck ; and here is — see, oh,
double T-O-N, which girls all
wear, like me; and here's a
heart, from cupid's dart, safe-
shielded by this corset's art.
This is my waist too tightly
laced on which
a bustle big
is placed.
This is my
dress. Its cost,
I guess, did my
poor papa much dis-
tress, because he sighed
when mamma tried it on,
and scolded so I cried;
but mamma said I soon would
wed and buy pa's clothes for him
instead. It's trimmed with lace
just in this place, 'neath which two
ankles show, with grace, in silken hose
to catch the beaus who think they're lovely,

I suppose.	These are
my f e e t	in slippers
neat, and	now if we
should chance to	meet we'll flirt
a l i t t l e on the	street. How sweet.

Anonymous.

[26]

THE STEGOMYIA

```
                I
                t
                s

                b
                i
                l
                l

               is
              long
           and wick-
             ed, and
               is
             filled
          with deadly
     juice        and              you
needn't   try     to      dodge   it  for   it
    won't         be              any use;
                  it
                 will
                chase
              you up
           and  catch
           you  and
          with woe will
          fill your cup;
          oh, the steg-
          omyia'll get
          you if you
          don't clean
               up
                !
```

                              Anonymous.

[27]

LITTLE BOYS TAKE WARNING

Two little boys, named Jack and Jim,
    In hot, or wintry weather,
No matter what the racket was
    Most always were together.

But one day Jack went to the stream
    To take a little swim;
He got a cramp, which laid him out,
    And here's the last of him:

Jim tackled the green-apple crop,
    And twenty-four he ate;
He got a cramp, which bent him so
    They couldn't jerk him straight.

Anonymous.

[28]

THE TALE OF A MOUSE *

" Fury said to
a mouse, That
he met
in the
house,
' Let us
both go
to law :
I will
prosecute
you.——
Come, I'll
take no
denial ;
We must
have a
trial :
For
really
this
morning
I've
nothing
to do.'
Said the
mouse to
the cur,
' Such a
trial,
dear sir,
With no
jury or
judge,
would be
wasting
our breath.'
' I'll be
judge,
I'll be
jury,'
Said
cunning
old Fury ;
' I'll try
the whole
cause,
and
condemn
you
to
death.' "

Lewis Carroll.

* By permission of the Macmillan Company.

[29]

THE MICE *

We lived beneath the mat,
　　Warm and snug and fat.
　　　　But one woe, and that
　　　　　　Was the cat!
　　　　　　　To our joys
　　　　　　　　a clog, In
　　　　　　　our eyes a
　　　　　　fog, On our
　　　　　hearts a log
　　　　Was the dog!
　　　When the
　　cat's away
Then
　the mice
　will
　　play.
　　　But, alas!
　　　　one day (so they say)
　　　　　　Came the dog and
　　　　　　　cat. Hunting
　　　　　　　　for a
　　　　　　　　rat
　　　　　　　Crushed
　　　　　　the mice
　　　　　all flat,
　　　　Each
　　　one
　　as
　　he
　　sat

Underneath the mat, Warm and snug and fat. Think of that.

Lewis Carroll.

* By permission of the Macmillan Company.

[30]

THE OLD LINE FENCE

ZIG–ZAGGING it went
   On the line of the farm,
      And the trouble it caused
         Was   often   quite   warm,
            The   Old   Line   Fence.
         It was changed every year
            By decree of the court,
      To which, when worn out,
   Our   sires   would   resort
With the Old Line Fence.
   In   hoeing   their   corn,
      When the sun, too, was hot,
         They   surely   would   jaw,
            Punch or claw, when they got
               To the Old Line Fence.
            In   dividing   the   lands
               It   fulfilled   no   desires,
         But answered quite well
   In   dividing   our   sires,
This   Old   Line   Fence.
   Though sometimes in this
      It would happen to fail,
         When, with top rail in hand,
            One would flare up and scale
               The   Old   Line   Fence!

Then the conflict was sharp
On   debatable   ground,
And the fertile soil there
Would be mussed far around
The   Old   Line   Fence.
It   was   shifted   so   oft
That no flowers there grew.
What frownings and clods,
And what words were shot
[through
The   Old   Line   Fence!
Our sires through the day
There would quarrel or fight,
With   a   vigor   or   vim,
But 'twas different at night
By   the   Old   Line   Fence.
The   fairest   maid   there
You   would   have   descried
That   ever   leaned   soft
On   the   opposite   side
Of   an   Old   Line   Fence.
Where our fathers built hate
There we builded our love,
Breathed our vows to be true
With our hands raised above
The   Old   Line   Fence.
Its place might be changed,
But there we would meet.
With our heads through the
[rails,
And with kisses most sweet,
At   the   Old   Line   Fence.

It was love made the change,
And the clasping of hands
Ending   ages   of   hate,
And between us now stands
Not a Sign of Line Fence.
No   debatable   ground
Now   enkindles   alarms.
I've the girl I met there,
And, well, both of the farms,
And   No   Line   Fence.
A. W. Bellaw.

JONES'S RIDE

The scenery was simply grand,
　　The day was one of bliss,
And so his auto, for a time,
　　Ran straight along like this.

The whatyoucallit snapped in two
　　When something went amiss,
And with a snort and sudden plunge

　　It　dug　a　hole　like　this.

Unsatisfied with lowly earth
　　It gave a screech and hiss,
And to the wonderment of Jones

It went
straight up
like this.

'Twas thus they vanished out of view
　　Above the gazing town;
The fifth verse of the poem shows
　　How much of both came down.
　　　　　　　　McLandburgh Wilson.

[34]

ON THE STREET

He bought a little block of stock
  The day he went to town;
And in the nature of such things,
          That
          Stock
          Went
          Right
          Straight
          Down!

    *   *   *   *

He sold a little block of stock:
  Now sorrow fills his cup,
For from the moment that he did,
          Up.
          Right
          Went
          Thing
          Blamed
          The

    *   *   *   *

He bought a little block of stock,
  Expecting he would taste of bliss;
He can't let go and can't hang on,

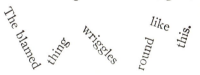

The blamed thing wriggles round like this.

                        Anonymous

AVOIRDUPOIS

The length of this line indicates the ton of coal as dug by the miner.
This one indicates the ton shipped to the dealer.
The small dealer gets a ton like this.
This is the one you pay for.
This is what you get.
The residue is:
Cinders and
Ashes.
And this line will give you some conception of the size of the BILL.

Anonymous.

A CUBIC TRIOLET

```
T H I S T R I O L E T
I S L I T T L E F U N
S O H A R D T O G E T
T H I S T R I O L E T
I N F U N A N D Y E T
E X A C T L Y D O N E
T H I S T R I O L E T
I S L I T T L E F U N
```

Anonymous.

[36]

ALPHABETICAL WHIMSEYS

THE SIEGE OF BELGRADE

AN Austrian army, awfully array'd,
    Boldly by battery besiege Belgrade;
    Cossack commanders cannonading come,
Deal devastation's dire destructive doom;
Ev'ry endeavour engineers essay,
For fame, for freedom, fight, fierce furious fray.
Gen'rals 'gainst gen'rals grapple,—gracious God!
How honors Heav'n heroic hardihood!
Infuriate, indiscriminate in ill,
Just Jesus, instant innocence instill!
Kinsmen kill kinsmen, kindred kindred kill.
Labour low levels longest, loftiest lines;
Men march 'midst mounds, motes, mountains, mur-
    d'rous mines.
Now noisy, noxious numbers notice nought,
Of outward obstacles o'ercoming ought;
Poor patriots perish, persecution's pest!
Quite quiet Quakers "Quarter, quarter," quest;
Reason returns, religion, right, redounds,
Suwarrow stop such sanguinary sounds!
Truce to thee, Turkey, terror to thy train!
Unwise, unjust, unmerciful Ukraine!
Vanish vile vengeance, vanish victory vain!

[37]

Why wish we warfare? wherefore welcome won
Xerxes, Xantippus, Xavier, Xenophon?
Yield, ye young Yaghier yeomen, yield your yell!
Zimmerman's, Zoroaster's, Zeno's zeal
Again attract; arts against arms appeal.
All, all ambitious aims, avaunt, away!
Et cetera, et cetera, et cetera.

Anonymous.

A, B, C

A IS an Angel of blushing eighteen:
    B is the Ball where the Angel was seen:
    C is her Chaperon, who cheated at cards:
D is the Deuxtemps, with Frank of the Guards:
E is her Eye, killing slowly but surely:
F is the Fan, whence it peeped so demurely:
G is the Glove of superlative kid:
H is the Hand which it spitefully hid:
I is the Ice which the fair one demanded:
J is the Juvenile, that dainty who handed:
K is the Kerchief, a rare work of art:
L is the Lace which composed the chief part:
M is the old Maid who watched the chits dance:
N is the Nose she turned up at each glance:
O is the Olga (just then in its prime):
P is the Partner who wouldn't keep time:
Q's the Quadrille, put instead of the Lanciers:
R's the Remonstrances made by the dancers:
S is the Supper where all went in pairs:
T is the Twaddle they talked on the stairs:

U is the Uncle who "thought we'd be goin'":
V is the Voice which his niece replied "No" in:
W is the Waiter, who sat up till eight:
X is his Exit, not rigidly straight:
Y is a Yawning fit caused by the Ball:
Z stands for Zero, or nothing at all.

C. S. Calverley.

MONORHYMED ALPHABET

A WAS an Army to settle disputes;
    B was a Bull, not the mildest of brutes;
    C was a Cheque, duly drawn upon Coutts;
D was King David, with harps and with lutes;
E was an Emperor, hailed with salutes;
F was a Funeral, followed by mutes;
G was a Gallant in Wellington boots;
H was a Hermit, and lived upon roots;
I was Justinian his Institutes;
K was a Keeper, who commonly shoots;
L was a Lemon, the sourest of fruits;
M was a Ministry—say Lord Bute's;
N was Nicholson, famous on flutes;
O was an Owl, that hisses and hoots;
P was a Pond, full of leeches and newts;
Q was a Quaker, in whitey-brown suits;
R was a Reason, which Paley refutes;
S was a Sergeant with twenty recruits;
T was Ten Tories with doubtful reputes;
U was Uncommonly bad cheroots;
V was Vicious motives, which malice imputes;

X was Ex-king driven out by emeutes;
Y is a Yawn; then, the last rhyme that suits;
Z is the Zuyder Zee, dwelt in by coots.

Anonymous.

MONORHYMED ALPHABET

A IS my Amy, so slender of waist;
B's little Bet, who my button replaced;
C is good Charlotte, good maker of paste;
D is Diana, the forest who traced;
E is plump Ellen, by Edward embraced;
F is poor Fanny, by freckles defaced;
G is Griselda, unfairly disgraced;
H is the Helen, who Ilion effaced;
I is fair Ida, that princess strait-laced;
J is the Judy, Punch finds to his taste;
K is Kate darling, by fond lovers chased;
L is Laurette, in coquetry encased;
M is pale Margaret, saintly and chaste;
N is gay Norah, o'er hills who has raced;
O is sweet Olive, a girl olive-faced;
P's pretty Patty, so daintily paced;
Q some fair Querist, in blue stockings placed;
R is frail Rose, from her true stem displaced;
S is brisk Sal, who a chicken can baste;
T is Theresa, at love who grimaced;
U is pure Una, that maid undebased;
V is Victoria, an empire who graced;
W is Winifred, time who will waste;
X is Xantippe, for scolding well braced;

Y's Mrs. Yelverton; ending in haste,
Z is Zenobia, in panoply cased.

Mortimer Collins.

MEMORANDUMS *

HAVE Angleworms attractive homes?
    Do Bumble-bees have brains?
   Do Caterpillars carry combs?
    Do Dodos dote on drains?
Can Eels elude elastic earls?
   Do Flatfish fish for flats?
Are Grigs agreeable to girls?
   Do Hares have hunting-hats?
Do Ices make an Ibex ill?
   Do Jackdaws jug their jam?
Do Kites kiss all the kids they kill?
   Do Llamas live on lamb?
Will Moles molest a mounted mink?
   Do Newts deny the news?
Are Oysters boisterous when they drink?
   Do parrots prowl in pews?
Do Quakers get their quills from quails?
   Do Rabbits rob on roads?
Are Snakes supposed to sneer at snails?
   Do Tortoises tease toads?
Can Unicorns perform on horns?
   Do vipers value veal?
Do Weasels weep when fast asleep?
   Can Xylophagans squeal?

* By permission of the Century Company.

Do Yaks in packs invite attacks?
Are Zebras full of zeal?

Charles E. Carryl.

AN ANIMAL ALPHABET

ALLIGATOR, beetle, porcupine, whale,
    Bobolink, panther, dragon-fly, snail,
    Crocodile, monkey, buffalo, hare,
Dromedary, leopard, mud-turtle, bear,
Elephant, badger, pelican, ox,
Flying-fish, reindeer, anaconda, fox,
Guinea-pig, dolphin, antelope, goose,
Humming-bird, weasel, pickerel, moose,
Ibex, rhinoceros, owl, kangaroo,
Jackal, opossum, toad, cockatoo,
Kingfisher, peacock, anteater, bat,
Lizard, ichneumon, honey-bee, rat,
Mocking-bird, camel, grasshopper, mouse,
Nightingale, spider, cuttle-fish, grouse,
Ocelot, pheasant, wolverine, auk,
Periwinkle, ermine, katydid, hawk,
Quail, hippopotamus, armadillo, moth,
Rattlesnake, lion, woodpecker, sloth,
Salamander, goldfinch, angleworm, dog,
Tiger, flamingo, scorpion, frog,
Unicorn, ostrich, nautilus, mole,
Viper, gorilla, basilisk, sole,
Whippoorwill, beaver, centipede, fawn,
Xantho, canary, polliwog, swan,

Yellowhammer, eagle, hyena, lark,
Zebra, chameleon, butterfly, shark.

Anonymous.

AN ANIMAL ALPHABET

A—The Absolutely Abstemious Ass,
   who resided in a Barrel, and only lived on
   Soda Water and Pickled Cucumbers.

B—The Bountiful Beetle,
   who always carried a Green Umbrella when
      it didn't rain,
   and left it at home when it did.

C—The Comfortable Confidential Cow,
   who sate in her Red Morocco Arm Chair and
   toasted her own Bread at the parlour Fire.

D—The Dolomphious Duck,
   who caught spotted frogs for her dinner
   with a Runcible Spoon.

E—The Enthusiastic Elephant,
   who ferried himself across the water with the
   Kitchen Poker and a New pair of Ear-rings.

F—The Fizzgiggious Fish,
   who always walked about upon Stilts,
   because he had no legs.

[43]

G—The Good-natured Gray Gull,
    who carried the Old Owl, and his Crimson
      Carpet-bag,
    across the river, because he could not swim.

H—The Hasty Higgeldipiggledy Hen,
    who went to market in a Blue Bonnet and
      Shawl,
    and bought a Fish for Supper.

I—The Inventive Indian,
    who caught a Remarkable Rabbit in a
    Stupendous Silver Spoon.

J—The Judicious Jubilant Jay,
    who did up her Back Hair every morning
      with a Wreath of Roses,
    Three feathers, and a Gold Pin.

K—The Kicking Kangaroo,
    who wore a Pale Pink Muslin dress
    with Blue spots.

L—The Lively Learned Lobster,
    who mended his own Clothes with
    a Needle and Thread.

M—The Melodious Meritorious Mouse,
    who played a merry minuet on the
    Piano-forte.

N—The Nutritious Newt,
   who purchased a Round Plum-pudding,
   for his granddaughter.

O—The Obsequious Ornamental Ostrich,
   who wore boots to keep his
   feet quite dry.

P—The Perpendicular Purple Polly,
   who read the Newspaper and ate Parsnip Pie
   with his Spectacles.

Q—The Queer Querulous Quail,
   who smoked a pipe of tobacco on the top of
   a Tin Tea-kettle.

R—The Rural Runcible Raven,
   who wore a White Wig and flew away
   with the Carpet Broom.

S—The Scroobious Snake,
   who always wore a Hat on his Head, for
   fear he should bite anybody.

T—The Tumultuous Tom-tommy Tortoise,
   who beat a Drum all day long in the
   middle of the wilderness.

U—The Umbrageous Umbrella-maker,
   whose Face nobody ever saw, because it was
   always covered by his Umbrella.

V—The Visibly Vicious Vulture,
   who wrote some verses to a Veal-cutlet in a
   Volume bound in Vellum.

W—The Worrying Whizzing Wasp,
   who stood on a Table, and played sweetly on a
   Flute with a Morning Cap.

X—The Excellent Double-extra XX
   imbibing King Xerxes, who lived a
   long while ago.

Y—The Yonghy-Bonghy-Bo,
   whose Head was ever so much bigger than his
   Body, and whose Hat was rather small.

Z—The Zigzag Zealous Zebra,
   who carried five Monkeys on his back all
   the way to Jellibolee.

                                    Edward Lear.

TYPOGRAPHICAL WHIMSEYS

DIRGE

To the memory of Miss Ellen Gee, of Kew, who died in consequence of being stung in the eye.

PEERLESS yet hapless maid of Q!
　　Accomplish'd LN G!
　Never again shall I and U
　　Together sip our T.

For, ah! the Fates, I know not Y,
　Sent 'midst the flowers a B,
Which ven'mous stung her in the I,
　So that she could not C.

LN exclaim'd, "Vile spiteful B!
　If ever I catch U
On jess'mine, rosebud, or sweet P,
　I'll change your stinging Q.

"I'll send you like a lamb or U
　Across th' Atlantic C.
From our delightful village Q
　To distant O Y E.

[47]

"A stream runs from my wounded I,
  Salt as the briny C
As rapid as the X or Y,
  The OIO or D.

"Then fare thee ill, insensate B!
  Who stung, nor yet knew Y,
Since not for wealthy Durham's C
  Would I have lost my I."

They bear with tears fair LN G
  In funeral R A,
A clay-cold corse now doom'd to B
  Whilst I mourn her DK.

Ye nymphs of Q, then shun each B,
  List to the reason Y;
For should A B C U at T,
  He'll surely sting your I.

Now in a grave L deep in Q,
  She's cold as cold can B,
Whilst robins sing upon A U
  Her dirge and LEG.

Anonymous.

O D V

Containing a Full, True, and Particular Account of the Terrible
Fate of Abraham Isaacs, of Ivy Lane.

IN I V Lane, of C T fame,
  There lived a man D C,
And A B I 6 was his name,
  Now mark his history.

Long time his conduct free from blame
  Did merit L O G,
Until an evil spirit came
  In the shape of O D V.

"O! that a man into his mouth
  Should put an N M E
To steal away his brains"—no drouth
  Such course from sin may free.

Well, A B drank, the O T Loon!
  And learned to swear, sans ruth;
And then he gamed, and U Z soon
  To D V 8 from truth.

An hourly glass with him was play,
  He'd swallow that with phlegm;
Judge what he'd M T in a day,
  "X P D Herculem."

Of virtue none to sots, I trow,
  With F E K C prate;
And 0 of N R G could now
  From A B M N 8.

Who on strong liquor badly dote,
  Soon poverty must know;
Thus A B in a C D coat
  Was shortly forced to go.

[49]

From poverty D C T he caught,
    And cheated not A F U,
For what he purchased paying 0,
    Or but an "I O U."

Or else when he had tried B 4,
    To shirk a debt, his wits,
He'd cry, "You shan't wait N E more.
    I'll W or quits."

So lost did I 6 now A P R,
    That said his wife, said she,
"F U act so, your fate quite clear
    Is for I 2 4 C."

His inside soon was out and out
    More fiery than K N;
And while his state was thereabout
    A cough C V R came.

He I P K Q N A tried,
    And linseed T and rue;
But 0 could save him, so he died
    As every 1 must 2.

Poor wight! till black i' the face he raved,
    'Twas P T S 2 C
His latest spirit "spirit" craved—
    His last words, "O D V."

[50]

MORAL

I'll not S A to preach and prate,
    But tell U if U do
Drink O D V at such R 8,
    Death will 4 stall U 2.

O U then who A Y Z have,
    Shun O D V as a wraith,
For 'tis a bonus to the grave,
    And S A unto death.

                  Anonymous.

AN ALPHABETICAL WOOING

L ET others talk of L N's eyes,
    And K T's figure light and free,
    Say L R, too, is beautiful—
        I heed them not while U I C.
U need not N V them, for U
    X L them all, my M L E.
I have no words when I would tell
    How much in love with U I B.
So sweet U R, my D R E,
    I love your very F E G;
And when you speak or sing, your voice
    Is like a winsome L O D.
When U R I C, hope D K's,
    I am a mere non- N T T.
Such F E K C has your smile,
    It shields from N E N M E.

For love so deep as mine, I fear,
  There is no other M E D.
But that you love me back again—
  O, thought of heavenly X T C;
So, lest my M T heart and I
  Should sing for love and L E G,
T's me no more—B Y's, B kind,
  O, M L E, U R, I C!

Anonymous.

O I C

I'M in a 10der mood to-day
    & feel poetic, 2;
  4 fun I'll just — off a line
    & send it off 2 U.

I'm sorry you've been 6 O long;
    Don't B disconsol8;
  But bear your ills with 42de,
    & they won't seem so gr8.

Anonymous.

THE ZEALLESS XYLOGRAPHER *

(Dedicated to the End of the Dictionary)

A XYLOGRAPHER started to cross the sea
    By means of a Xanthic Xebec;
  But, alas! he sighed for the Zuyder Zee,
    And feared he was in for a wreck.

* By permission of the Century Company.

[52]

He tried to smile, but all in vain,
  Because of a Zygomatic pain;
And as for singing, his cheeriest tone
  Reminded him of a Xylophone—
Or else, when the pain would sharper grow,
  His notes were as keen as a Zuffolo.
And so it is likely he did not find
  On board Xenodochy to his mind.
The fare was poor, and he was sure
  Xerophagy he could not endure;
Zoöphagous surely he was, I aver,
  This dainty and starving Xylographer.
Xylophagous truly he could not be—
  No sickly vegetarian he!
He'd have blubbered like any old Zeuglodon
  Had Xerophthalmia not come on.
And the end of it was he never again
  In a Xanthic Xebec went sailing the main.
                              Mary Mapes Dodge

A GEOGRAPHICAL LOVE SONG

I N the State of Mass.
    There lived a lass,
      I love to go N. C.;
No other Miss.
Can e'er, I Wis.,
    Be half so dear to Me.
R. I. is blue
And her cheeks the hue
    Of shells where waters swash;

On her pink-white phiz.
There Nev. Ariz.
   The least complexion Wash.
La.! could I win
The heart of Minn.,
   I'd ask for nothing more,
But I only dream
Upon the theme,
   And Conn. it o'er and Ore.
Why is it, pray,
I can't Ala.
   This love that makes me Ill.?
N. Y., O., Wy.
Kan. Nev. Ver. I
   Propose to her my will?
I shun the task
'Twould be to ask
   This gentle maid to wed.
And so, to press
My suit, I guess
   Alaska Pa. instead.   *Anonymous.*

THE SUNDAY FISHERMAN

A FISHERMAN, on angling bent,
  One Sabbath morning left his tent.

    The Tent, Λ

He took his can, and very quick
He dug his fish-worms with a pick.

    The Pick, (——   The Worms, ς ς

[54]

He thought he'd try for bass and smelt,
And fixed his fish-bag to his belt.

The Belt, ○   The Bag, ○

In case some fish of size he'd get,
He took along his landing-net.

The Landing-Net, ⊐

As fishermen get very dry,
They always have a flask hard by.

The Flask, ⋀

As fishermen get hungry, too,
Of pretzels he procured a few.

The Pretzels, ⅋ ⅋ ⅋ ⅋

Some lines he took along on spools
To teach them to the finny schools.

The Spools, ▭ ▭ ▭

He had some entertaining books
Of highly-tempered Limerick hooks.

The Hooks, J J J

And thus prepared, he got his boat,
And out upon the stream did float.

The Boat, ⏝

Whene'er the wind began to fail
He used the paddle with the sail.

The Paddle, ⊲⊃

He stopped to fish, among the sedge,
A mile or so below the bridge.

The Bridge, ⊓⊓⊓⊓⊓⊓⊳

Some bites he straight began to get,
It was the gallinippers bit.

The Gallinippers, ⋈   ⋈   ⋈

One of his lines spun off the reel;
He landed in the boat an eel.

The Eel, ᴄᴐ

Then quickly it began to rain,
But his umbrella was in vain.

The Umbrella, ⌒|

Above his head the thunder crashed,
And all around the lightning flashed.

The Lightning, ⌐

The storm blew, and the boat upset;
The man went down into the wet.

The Upturned Boat ⌓

[56]

And as he sank, his bubbles rose,
Smaller and smaller toward the close.

The Bubbles, O o o o

Oh, Sunday fishers, old and young,
You will get drowned, or you'll get hung!

The Gallows, ⌐

. *W. Bellaw.*

AN ARAB AND HIS DONKEY

A N Arab came to the river side,
    With a donkey bearing an obelisk;
  But he would not try to ford the tide,
    For he had too good an *.

Boston Globe.

*   *   *

So he camped all night by the river side,
  And he remained till the tide ceased to swell,
For he knew should the donkey from life subside,
  He never would find its ||.

Salem Sunbeam.

*   *   *

When the morning dawned, and tide was out,
  The pair crossed over 'neath Allah's protection;
And the Arab was happy, we have no doubt,
  For he had the best donkey in all that §.

Somerville Journal.

[57]

You are wrong, they were drowned in crossing over,
  Though the donkey was bravest of all his race;
He luxuriates now in horse-heaven clover,
  And his master has gone to the Prophet's #.
                              Elevated Railway Journal.

                    *   *   *

These asinine poets deserved to be "blowed,"
  Their rhymes being faulty and frothy and beery;
What really befell the ass and its load
  Will ever remain a desolate ?.
                              Paper and Print.

                    *   *   *

Our Yankee friends, with all their ——
  For once, we guess, their mark have missed;
And with poetry Paper and Print is rash
  In damming its flow with its editor's ☞

In parable and moral leave a between,
  For reflection, or your wits fall out of joint;
The "Arab," ye see, is a printing machine,
  And the donkey is he who can't see the .
                              British and Colonial Printer.

A SONG OF THE &

O F all the types in a printer's hand
    Commend me to the ampersand,
    For he's the gentleman (seems to me)
    Of the typographical companie.

[58]

O my nice little ampersand,
My graceful, swanlike ampersand!
Nothing that Cadmus ever planned
Equals my elegant ampersand!

Many a letter your writers hate,
Ugly Q, with its tail so straight,
X, that makes you cross as a bear,
And Z, that helps you with "zounds" to swear.
    But not my nice little ampersand,
    My easily dashed off ampersand;
    Any odd shape folks understand
    To mean my Protean ampersand.

Nothing for him that's starch or stiff;
Never he's used in scold or tiff;
State epistles, so dull and so grand,
Mustn't contain the shortened "and."
    No, my nice little ampersand,
    You are good for those who're jolly and bland;
    In days when letters were dried with sand,
    Old frumps wouldn't use my ampersand.

But he is dear in old friendship's call,
Or when love is laughing through lady scrawl,
"Come & dine & have bachelor's fare,"
"Come & I'll keep you a round & square."
    Yes, my nice little ampersand
    Never must into a word expand;
    Gentle sign of affection stand,
    My kind, familiar ampersand.

Anonymous.

[59]

LOVELILTS

THINE eyes, dear one, dot dot, are like, dash,
    what?
    They, pure as sacred oils, bless and anoint
    My sin-swamped soul which at thy feet
      sobs out,
    O exclamation point, O point, O point!

Ah, had I words, blank blank, which, dot, I've not,
I'd swoon in songs which should'st illume the dark
With light of thee. Ah, God (it's *strong* to swear)
Why, why, interrogation mark, why, mark?

Dot dot dot dot. And so, dash, yet, but nay!
My tongue takes pause; some words must not be
    said,
For fear the world, cold hyphen eyed, austere,
Should'st shake thee by the throat till reason
    fled.

One hour of love we've had. Dost thou recall
Dot dot dash blank interrogation mark?
The night was ours, blue heaven over all
Dash, God! dot stars, keep thou our secret dark!

                              Anonymous.

ROMANTIC RECOLLECTIONS

I

WHEN I lay in a cradle and suck'd a coral,
    I lov'd romance in my childish way;
    And stories, with or without a moral,
       Were welcome as ever the flow'rs in May.
For love of the false I learnt
    my spelling,
  And brav'd the perils of—
While matters of fact were
    most repelling,
  Romance was pleasant as aught could—

II

My reading took me to desert islands,
  And buried me deep in Arabian Nights;
Sir Walter led me amongst the Highlands,
  Or into the thickest of Moslem fights.
I found the elder Dumas delightful—
  Before the son had eclips'd the—
And Harrison Ainsworth finely
    frightful,
  And Fenimore Cooper far from—

III

A few years later I took to reading
  The morbid stories of Edgar Poe—
Not healthy viands for youthful feeding
  (And all my advisers told me so).

But, healthy or not, I enjoy'd them
    vastly;
  My feverish fancy was nightly—
Upon horrible crimes and murders
    ghastly
  Which sent me terrified off to—

IV

Well; what with perils upon the prairies,
  And haunted ruins and ghosts in white,
And wars with giants and gifts from fairies,
  At last I came to be craz'd outright.
And many a time, in my nightly
    slumbers,
  Bearing a glove as a lady's—
I held the lists against countless
    numbers,
  After the style of the darkest—

V

I am chang'd at present; the olden fever
  Has left my brain in a sounder state;
In commonplace I'm a firm believer,
  And hunt for figure and fact and date.
I have lost a lot of my old affection,
  For books on which I was wont to—
But still I can thrill at the recol-
    lection
  Of mystery, magic, and martial—

Henry S. Leigh.

[62]

LIPOGRAMS *

FOUR LIPOGRAMS

THE RUSSO-TURKISH WAR

WAR harms all ranks, all arts, all crafts appal;
    At Mars' harsh blast arch, rampart, altar
        fall!
Ah! hard as adamant a braggart Czar
Arms vassal-swarms, and fans a fatal war!
Rampant at that bad call, a Vandal band
Harass, and harm, and ransack Wallach-land.
A Tartar phalanx Balkan's scarp hath past,
And Allah's standard falls, alas! at last.

THE FALL OF EVE

EVE, Eden's empress, needs defended be;
    The Serpent greets her when she seeks the
        tree.
Serene she sees the speckled tempter creep;
Gentle he seems—perverted schemer deep—

---

* Poems so constructed as to omit entirely a certain letter, or, on
the contrary, restricted to the use of but one vowel.

[63]

Yet endless pretexts, ever fresh, prefers,
Perverts her senses, revels when she errs,
Sneers when she weeps, regrets, repents she fell,
Then, deep-revenged, reseeks the nether Hell!

THE APPROACH OF EVENING

IDLING I sit in this mild twilight dim,
Whilst birds, in wild swift vigils, circling skim.
Light wings in sighing sink, till, rising bright,
Night's Virgin Pilgrim swims in vivid light.

INCONTROVERTIBLE FACTS

NO monk too good to rob, or cog, or plot,
No fool so gross to bolt Scotch collops hot.
From Donjon tops no Oronooko rolls.
Logwood, not lotos, floods Oporto's bowls.
Troops of old tosspots oft to sot consort.
Box tops our schoolboys, too, do flog for sport.
No cool monsoons blow oft on Oxford dons,
Orthodox, jog-trot, book-worm Solomons!
Bold Ostrogoths of ghosts no horror show.
On London shop-fronts no hop-blossoms grow.
To crocks of gold no Dodo looks for food.
On soft cloth footstools no old fox doth brood.
Long storm-tost sloops forlorn do work to port.
Rooks do not roost on spoons, nor woodcocks snort.
Nor dog on snowdrop or on coltsfoot rolls,
Nor common frog concocts long protocols.

Anonymous.

[64]

PHILOSOPHY

DULL humdrum murmurs lull, but hubbub
stuns.
Lucullus snuffs up musk, mundungus shuns.
Puss purs, buds burst, bucks butt, luck turns up
trumps;
But full cups, hurtful, spur up unjust thumps.

Anonymous

THE FATE OF NASSAN *

BOLD Nassan quits his caravan,
A hazy mountain grot to scan;
Climbs jaggy rocks to spy his way,
Doth tax his sight, but far doth stray.

Not work of man, nor sport of child,
Finds Nassan in that mazy wild;
Lax grow his joints, limbs toil in vain—
Poor wight! why didst thou quit that plain.

Vainly for succour Nassan calls,
Know, Zillah, that thy Nassan falls;
But prowling wolf and fox may joy,
To quarry on thy Arab boy.

Anonymous

* E is omitted.

[65]

ALPHABET VERSE *

G OD gives the grazing ox his meat,
 And quickly hears the sheep's low cry,
But man, who tastes his finest wheat,
 Should joy to lift his praises high.

Anonymous

* This stanza includes all the letters of the alphabet.

ALLITERATIVE WHIMSEYS

MY MADELINE

MY Madeline! my Madeline!
　　Mark my melodious midnight moans
　Much may my melting music mean,
　　My modulated monotones.

My mandolin's mild minstrelsy,
　My mental music magazine,
My mouth, my mind, my memory,
　Must mingling murmur "Madeline."

Muster 'mid midnight masquerades,
　Mark Moorish maidens', matrons' mien,
'Mongst Murcia's most majestic maids
　Match me my matchless Madeline.

Mankind's malevolence may make
　Much melancholy music mine;
Many my motives may mistake,
　My modest merits much malign.

My Madeline's most mirthful mood
　Much mollifies my mind's machine;
My mournfulness' magnitude
　Melts—makes me merry—Madeline'

Match-making mas may machinate,
  Manœuvring misses me misween;
Mere money may make many mate;
  My magic motto's, "Madeline!"

Melt, most mellifluous melody,
  Midst Murcia's misty mounts marine,
Meet me 'mid moonlight—marry me,
  Madonna mia!—my Madeline!

Anonymous.

BLOOM, BEAUTEOUS BLOSSOMS

BLOOM, beauteous blossoms, budding bow-
      ers beneath!
    Behold, Boreas' bitter blast by brief
  Bright beams becalmed; balmy breezes
      breathe,
      Banishing blight, bring bliss beyond be-
      lief.

Build, bonny birds! By bending birchen bough,
  By bush, by beech, by buttressed branches bare,
By bluebell-brightened bramble-brake; bestow
  Bespeckled broods; but bold bad boys beware!

Babble, blithe brooklet! Barren borders breach,
  Bathe broomy banks, bright buttercups bedew,
Briskly by bridge, by beetling bluff, by beach,
  Beckoned by bravely bounding billows blue!

Sir Patrick Fells.

[68]

SUSAN SIMPSON

SUDDEN swallows swiftly skimming,
    Sunset's slowly spreading shade,
  Silvery songsters sweetly singing,
    Summer's soothing serenade.

Susan Simpson strolled sedately,
    Stifling sobs, suppressing sighs.
  Seeing Stephen Slocum, stately
    She stopped, showing some surprise.

"Say," said Stephen, "sweetest sigher;
    Say, shall Stephen spouseless stay?"
  Susan, seeming somewhat shyer,
    Showed submissiveness straightway.

Summer's season slowly stretches,
    Susan Simpson Slocum she—
  So she signed some simple sketches—
    Soul sought soul successfully.

  .   .   .   .   .

Six Septembers Susan swelters;
    Six sharp seasons snow supplies;
  Susan's satin sofa shelters
    Six small Slocums side by side.

Anonymous.

THE CUSHAT

THE cushat croods, the corbie cries,
 The cuckoo conks, the prattling pies
  To geck there they begin;
The jargon of the jangling jays,
The cracking craws and keckling jays,
 They deav'd me with their din;
The painted pawn, with Argus eyes,
 Can on his May-cock call,
The turtle wails on wither'd trees,
 And echo answers all.
  Repeating with greeting,
   How fair Narcissus fell,
  By lying and spying
   His shadow in the well.

The air was sober, saft, and sweet,
Nae misty vapours, wind, nor weet,
 But quiet, calm, and clear;
To foster Flora's fragrant flowers.
Whereon Apollo's paramours
 Had trinkled mony a tear;
The which, like silver shakers, shined,
 Embroidering Beauty's bed,
Wherewith their heavy heads declined
 In Maye's colours clad;
  Some knopping, some dropping
   Of balmy liquor sweet,
  Excelling and smelling
   Through Phœbus' wholesome heat.
    Alexander Montgomery.

[70]

QUÆRITUR

DAWN that disheartens the desolate dunes,
  Dulness of day as it bursts on the beach,
  Sea-wind that shrillest the thinnest of tunes,
    What is the wisdom thy wailings would
      teach?
Far, far away, down the foam-frescoed reach,
  Where ravening rocks cleave the crest of the
    seas,
Sigheth the sound of thy sonorous speech,
  As grey gull and guillemot gather their fees;
  Taking toll of the beasts that are bred in the
    as.

Foam-flakes fly farther than faint eyes can follow—
  Drop down the desolate dunes and are done;
Fleeter than foam-flowers flitteth the Swallow,
  Sheer for the sweets of the South and the Sun:
What is thy tale, O thou treacherous Swallow?
  Sing me thy secret, Beloved of the Skies,
That I may gather my garments and follow—
  Flee on the path of thy pinions and rise
  Where strong storms cease and the weary wind
    dies.

Lo! I am bound with the chains of my sorrow;
  Swallow, swift Swallow, ah, wait, for a while!
Stay but a moment—it may be to-morrow
  Chains shall be severed and sad souls shall smile!

[71]

Only a moment—a mere minute's measure—
How shall it hurt such a swift one as thou?
Pitiless Swallow, full flushed for thy pleasure,
  Canst thou not even one instant allow
  To weaker-winged wanderers? Wait for me now!
                              Rudyard Kipling.

PROCURATORES

OH, vestment of velvet and virtue,
    Oh, venomous victors of vice,
      Who hurt men who never have hurt you,
        Oh, calm, cold, crueller than ice!
Why wilfully wage you this war? Is
  All pity purged out of your breast?
Oh, purse-prigging procuratores,
        Oh, pitiless pest!

We had smote and made redder than roses,
    With juice not of fruit nor of bud,
The truculent townspeople's noses,
    And bathed brutal butchers in blood;
And we all aglow in our glories,
    Heard you not in the deafening din;
And ye came, O ye procuratores,
        And ran us all in!
                        From the Shotover Papers.

ACROSTICS

ACROSTIC

Earth now is green and heaven is blue;
Lively spring which makes all new,
Iolly spring doth enter.
Sweet young sunbeams do subdue
Angry aged winter.
Blasts are mild and seas are calm,
Every meadow flows with balm,
The earth wears all her riches,
Harmonious birds sing such a psalm
As ear and heart bewitches.

Reserve (sweet spring) this nymph of ours,
Eternal garlands of thy flowers,
Green garlands never wasting;
In her shall last our state's fair spring,
Now and forever flourishing,
As long as heaven is lasting.

Sir John Davies.

ACROSTIC

Go, little poem, and present
Respectful terms of compliment,
A Gentle Lady bids thee speak;
Courteous is She, though Thou be weak.
Evoke from Heav'n, as thick as Manna,

[73]

Joy after joy, on Grace Joanna.
On Fornham's glebe and pasture land
A blessing pray. Long, long may stand,
Not touch'd by time, the Rectory blithe.
No grudging churl dispute his tithe.
At Easter be the offerings due

With cheerful spirit paid. Each pew
In decent order fill'd. No noise
Loud intervene to drown the voice,
Learning or wisdom, of the Teacher.
Impressive be the Sacred Preacher,
And strict his notes on Holy Page.
May young and old from age to age
Salute and still point out the "Good Man's Parson-
   age."

Charles Lamb.

ACROSTIC

Lovely and loved, o'er the unconquered brave
Your charms resistless, matchless girl, shall reign,
Dear as the mother holds her infant's grave,
In Love's warm regions, warm, romantic Spain.
And should your fate to courts your steps ordain,

Kings would in vain to regal pomp appeal,
And lordly bishops kneel to you in vain,
Nor Valour's fire, Love's power, nor Churchman's
   zeal
Endure 'gainst Love's (time's up) untarnished
   steel.

Bogart.

[74]

ACROSTIC *

"**A**re you deaf, Father William?" the young man said,
"**D**id you hear what I told you just now?
"**E**xcuse me for shouting! Don't waggle your head
"**L**ike a blundering, sleepy old cow!
"**A** little maid dwelling in Wallington Town,
"**I**s my friend, so I beg to remark;
"**D**o you think she'd be pleased if a book were sent
     down
"**E**ntitled 'The Hunt of the Snark?' "

"**P**ack it up in brown paper!" the old man cried,
"**A**nd seal it with olive-and-dove.
"**I** command you to do it!" he added with pride,
"**N**or forget, my good fellow, to send her beside
"**E**aster Greetings, and give her my love."

Lewis Carroll.

AN ACROSTIC

Friendship, thou'rt false! I hate thy flattering smile!
Return to me those years I spent in vain.
In early youth the victim of thy guile,
Each joy took wing ne'er to return again,—
Ne'er to return; for, chilled by hopes deceived,
Dully the slow-paced hours now move along;
So changed the times when thoughtless I believed
Her honeyed words, and heard her siren song.
If e'er, as me, she lure some youth to stray,
Perhaps, before too late, he'll listen to my lay.

Anonymous.

* By permission of the Macmillan Company.

[75]

AN ACROSTIC *

A boat, beneath a sunny sky
Lingering onward dreamily
In an evening of July—

Children three that nestle near,
Eager eye and willing ear,
Pleased a simple tale to hear—

Long has paled that sunny sky:
Echoes fade and memories die:
Autumn frosts have slain July.

Still she haunts me, phantomwise,
Alice, moving under skies
Never seen by waking eyes.

Children, yet, the tale to hear,
Eager eye and willing ear,
Lovingly shall nestle near.

In a Wonderland they lie,
Dreaming as the days go by,
Dreaming as the summers die;

Ever drifting down the stream—
Lingering in the golden gleam—
Life, what is it but a dream?

Lewis Carroll.

* By permission of the Macmillan Company.

DOUBLE ACROSTIC

Unite and untie are the same—so say yo**u**.
Not in wedlock, I ween, has the unity bee**n**.
In the drama of marriage, each wandering gou**t**
To a new face would fly—all except you and **I**
Each seeking to alter the spell in their scen**e**.

Anonymous.

PECULIAR ACROSTIC

A Valentine

*(Read the first letter of the first line, second letter
of the second line, and so on.)*

FOR her this rhyme is penned, whose lum-
          inous eyes,
      Brightly expressive as the twins of Leda,
Shall find her own sweet name, that nestling lies
Upon the page, enwrapped from every reader.
Search narrowly the lines!—they hold a treasure
Divine—a talisman—an amulet
That must be worn at heart. Search well the
          measure—
The words—the syllables! Do not forget
The trivialest point, or you may lose your labour!
And yet there is in this no Gordian knot
Which one might not undo without a sabre,
If one could merely comprehend the plot.

[77]

Enwritten upon the leaf where now are peering
Eye's scintillating soul, there lie perdus
Three eloquent words oft uttered in the hearing
Of poets by poets—as the name is a poet's, too,
Its letters, although naturally lying
Like the Knight Pinto—Mendez Ferdinando—
Still form a synonym for Truth. Cease trying!
You will not read the riddle, though you do the
    best you can do!

Edgar Allan Poe.

PARTICULAR ACROSTIC

Though crost in our affections, still the flames
Of Honour shall secure our noble Names;
Nor shall Our fate divorce our faith, Or cause
The least Mislike of love's Diviner lawes.
Crosses sometimes Are cures, Now let us prove,
That no strength Shall Abate the power of love:
Honour, wit, beauty, Riches, wise men call
Frail fortune's Badges, In true love lies all.
Therefore to him we Yield, our Vowes shall be
Paid — Read, and written in Eternity:
That All may know when men grant no Redress,
Much love can sweeten the unhappinesS.

Thomas Jordan.

ENIGMAS AND CHARADES

ENIGMA ON THE LETTER H

'TWAS whispered in heaven, 'twas muttered in
    hell,
    And echo caught faintly the sound as it fell;
On the confines of earth 'twas permitted to rest,
And the depths of the ocean its presence confessed;
'Twill be found in the sphere when 'tis riven
    asunder,
Be seen in the lightning, and heard in the thunder.
'Twas allotted to man with his earliest breath,
It assists at his birth and attends him in death,
Presides o'er his happiness, honor, and health,
Is the prop of his house and the end of his wealth,
In the heaps of the miser is hoarded with care,
But is sure to be lost in his prodigal heir.
It begins every hope, every wish it must bound,
It prays with the hermit, with monarchs is crowned;
Without it the soldier, the sailor, may roam,
But woe to the wretch who expels it from home.
In the whisper of conscience 'tis sure to be found,
Nor e'en in the whirlwind of passion is drowned;
'Twill soften the heart, but, though deaf to the ear,
It will make it acutely and instantly hear;

But, in short, let it rest like a delicate flower;
Oh, breathe on it softly, it dies in an hour.

Catherine Fanshawe.

TRAVESTY OF MISS FANSHAWE'S ENIGMA

I DWELLS in the Hearth, and I breathes in
    the Hair;
If you searches the Hocean, you'll find that
    I'm there.
The first of all Hangels in Holympus am Hi,
Yet I'm banished from 'Eaven, expelled from on
    'igh.
But, though on this Horb I'm destined to grovel,
I'm ne'er seen in an 'Ouse, in an 'Ut, nor an 'Ovel.
Not an 'Orse, not an 'Unter e'er bears me, alas!
But often I'm found on the top of a Hass.
I resides in a Hattic, and loves not to roam,
And yet I'm invariably absent from 'Ome.
Though 'Ushed in the 'Urricane, of the Hatmo-
    sphere part,
I enters no 'Ed, I creeps into no 'Art.
Only look, and you'll see in the Heye Hi appear;
Only 'Ark, and you'll 'Ear me just breathe in the
    Hear.
Though in sex not an 'E, I am (strange paradox)
Not a bit of an 'Effer, but partly a Hox.
Of Heternity I'm the beginning! and, mark,
Though I goes not with Noar, I'm first in the Hark.

I'm never in 'Ealth, have with Fysic no power,
I dies in a month, but comes back in a Hour.
Horace Mayhew.

THE LETTER H'S PROTEST TO THE COCKNEYS

WHEREAS by you I have been driven
From 'ouse, from 'ome, from 'ope, from
'eaven,
And placed by your most learned society
In Hexile, Hanguish, and Hanxiety,
Nay, charged without one just pretence
With Harrogance and Himpudence,—
I here demand full restitution,
And beg you'll mend your Hellocution.
Mr. Skeat.

ENIGMA ON THE LETTER I

I AM not in youth, nor in manhood or age,
But in infancy ever am known.
I'm a stranger alike to the fool and the sage,
And though I'm distinguished on history's page,
I always am greatest alone.

I'm not in the earth, nor the sun, nor the moon;
You may search all the sky, I'm not there;
In the morning and evening, though not in the noon,
You may plainly perceive me, for, like a balloon,
I am always suspended in air.

[81]

Though disease may possess me, and sickness, and
    pain,
   I am never in sorrow or gloom.
Though in wit and in wisdom I equally reign,
I'm the heart of all sin, and have long lived in vain,
   Yet I ne'er shall be found in the tomb.
                   Catherine Fanshawe.

AN UNSOLVED ENIGMA

THE noblest object in the works of art,
    The brightest scenes which nature can im-
       part;
The well-known signal in the time of peace,
The point essential in a tenant's lease;
The farmer's comfort as he drives the plough,
A soldier's duty, and a lover's vow;
A contract made before the nuptial tie,
A blessing riches never can supply;
A spot that adds new charms to pretty faces,
An engine used in fundamental cases;
A planet seen between the earth and sun,
A prize that merit never yet has won;
A loss which prudence seldom can retrieve,
The death of Judas, and the fall of Eve;
A part between the ankle and the knee,
A papist's toast and a physician's fee;
A wife's ambition and a parson's dues,
A miser's idol, and the badge of Jews.
If now your happy genius can divine
A corresponding word for every line,

By the first letters plainly may be found
An ancient city that is much renowned.
Anna Seward.

AN UNSOLVED ENIGMA

I SIT stern as a rock when I'm raising the wind,
   But the storm once abated, I'm gentle and
      kind.
I have Kings at my feet, who await but my nod
To kneel down in the dust on the ground I have
   trod.
Though seen by the world, I am known but to few;
The Gentile deserts me, I am pork to the Jew.
I have never passed but one night in the dark,
And that was like Noah, alone in the ark.
My weight is three pounds, my length is one mile,
And when you have guessed me, you'll say with a
   smile
That my first and my last are the best of this isle.
Anonymous.

AN UNSOLVED ENIGMA

I'M the stoutest of voices in Orchestra heard,
   And yet in an Orchestra never have been.
   I'm a bird of bright plumage, yet less like a
      bird
Nothing in nature ever was seen.

Touching earth I expire, in water I die,
In air I lose breath, yet can swim and can fly.
Darkness destroys me, and light is my death;
You can't keep me alive without stopping my
    breath.
If my name can't be guessed by a boy or a man,
By a girl or a woman it certainly can.

Anonymous.

OLD RIDDLE *

GOD made Adam out of dust;
    But thought it best to make me first.
    And I was made before the man
According to God's holy plan.
My body he did make complete;
But without arms, or legs, or feet.
My ways and actions did control
And I was made without a soul.
A living creature I became;
'Twas Adam that gave me my name.
Then from his presence I withdrew;
Nor more of Adam ever knew.
I did my Maker's laws obey:
From them I never went astray;
Thousands of miles I roam in fear;
But seldom on the land appear.
But God in me did something see,
And put a living soul in me.
A soul in me the Lord did claim,
And took from me that soul again.

* Answer: The whale that swallowed Jonah.

And when from me that soul was fled,
I was the same as when first made.
And without arms, or legs, or soul,
I travel now from pole to pole;
I labor hard both day and night;
To fallen men I give great light.
Thousands of people young and old,
Do by my death great light behold.
No fear of death doth trouble me,
Nor happiness I cannot see.
To heaven above I ne'er shall go;—
Nor to the grave, nor hell below.
The Scriptures I cannot believe
Whether right or wrong I can't conceive
Although my name therein is found
They are to me an empty sound.
And when friends these lines do read
Go search the Scriptures with all speed,
And if my name you can't find there,
It will be strange—I do declare.

Anonymous.

A FAMOUS RIDDLE *

COME and commiserate
One who was blind,
Homeless and desolate,
Void of a mind;
Guileless, deceiving,
Through unbelieving,

* Answer: See I Samuel xix. 13

Free from all sin;
By mortals adored,
Still I ignored
The world I was in.
King Ptolemy's, Cæsar's
And Tiglath-pileser's
Birthdays are shown;
Wise men, astrologers,
All are acknowledgers,
Mine is unknown,
I ne'er had a father
Or mother; or rather,
If I had either,
Then they were neither
Alive at my birth;
Lodged in a palace,
Hunted by malice,
I did not inherit
By lineage or merit
A spot on the earth.
Nursed among pagans,
No one baptized me,
A sponsor I had
Who ne'er catechised me;
She gave me the name
To her heart was the dearest,
She gave me the place
To her bosom was nearest;
But one look of kindness
She cast on me never,
Nor a word in my blindness
I heard from her ever.

Compassed by dangers,
Nothing could harm me;
By foemen and strangers,
Naught could alarm me;
I saved, I destroyed;
I blessed, I annoyed;
Kept a crown for a Prince,
But had none of my own;
Filled the place of a King,
But ne'er sat on a throne;
Rescued a warrior; baffled a plot;
Was what I seemed not,
Seemed what I was not;
Devoted to slaughter,
A price on my head,
A King's lovely daughter
Watched by my bed;
Though gently she dressed me,
Fainting with fear,
She never caressed me
Nor wiped off a tear,
Never moistened my lips
Though parching and dry
(What marvel a blight
Should pursue till she die!)
'Twas royalty nursed me,
Wretched and poor;
'Twas royalty cursed me
In secret, I'm sure.
I live not, I died not;
But tell you I must
That ages have passed

[87]

Since I first turned to dust.
This paradox whence?
This squalor! This splendor!
Say! was I a King,
Or a silly pretender?
Fathom the mystery,
Deep in my history!
Was I a man?
An angel supernal?
A demon infernal?
Solve it who can!

Anonymous

OLD RIDDLE *

IF it be true, as Welshmen say,
   Honor depends on pedigree,
   Then stand by—clear the way—
And let me have fair play.
For, though you boast thro' ages dark
Your pedigree from Noah's ark,
I, too, was with him there.
For I was Adam, Adam I,
And I was Eve, and Eve was I,
In spite of wind and weather;
But, mark me—Adam was not I,
Neither was Mrs. Adam I,
Unless they were together.
Suppose, then, Eve and Adam talking—
With all my heart, but if they're walking
There ends all simile,

* Answer : A bedfellow.

For, tho' I've tongue and often talk,
And tho' I've feet, yet when I walk
There is an end of me!
Not such an end but I have breath,
Therefore to such a kind of death
I have but small objection.
I may be Turk, I may be Jew,
And tho' a Christian, yet 'tis true
I die by resurrection!

Anonymous.

ENIGMA ON COD

CUT off my head, and singular I act,
    Cut off my tail, and plural I appear;
    Cut off my head and tail, and, wondrous fact,
        Although my middle's left, there's nothing
        there.
What is my head cut off? A sounding sea;
    What is my tail cut off? A flowing river,
In whose translucent depths I fearless play,
    Parent of sweetest sounds, yet mute forever.

Anonymous.

CHARADE *

COME from my First, ay, come;
    The battle dawn is nigh,
    And the screaming trump and the thun-
    dering-drum
    Are calling thee to die.

* Campbell.

[89]

Fight, as thy father fought;
  Fall, as thy father fell:
Thy task is taught, thy shroud is wrought;
  So forward and farewell!

Toll ye my Second, toll;
  Fling high the flambeau's light;
And sing the hymn for a parted soul
  Beneath the silent night;
The helm upon his head,
  The cross upon his breast,
Let the prayer be said, and the tear be shed:
  Now take him to his rest!

Call ye my Whole, go call
  The lord of lute and lay,
And let him greet the sable pall
  With a noble song to-day;
Ay, call him by his name,
  No fitter hand may crave
To light the flame of a soldier's fame
  On the turf of a soldier's grave!
                    Winthrop Mackworth Praed.

ANAGRAMS

A TELEGRAM ANAGRAMMATISED

THOUGH but a *late germ*, with a wondrous
    elation,
    Yet like a *great elm* it o'ershadows each
      station,
Et malgré the office is still a large free mart,
So joyous the crowd was, you'd thought it a *glee
    mart ;*
But they raged at no news from the nations bellig-
    erent,
And I said, *Let'm rage*, since the air is refrigerant.
I then met large numbers, whose drink was not
    sherbet,
Who scarce could look up when their eyes the gas-
    glare met ;
So when I had learned from commercial adviser,
That *mere galt* for sand was the great fertiliser,
I bade *Mr. Eaglet*, although 'twas ideal,
Get some from the clay-pit, and so *get'm real ;*
Then, just as my footstep was leaving the portal,
I met an *elm targe* on a great Highland mortal,
With the maid he had wooed by the loch's flowery
    margelet,
And rowed in his boat, which for rhyme's sake call
    bargelet,

And blithe to the breeze would have set the sail
   daily,
But it blew at that rate which our sailors *term gale*,
   aye;
I stumbled against the fair bride he had married,
When a *merle gat* at large from a cage that she car-
   ried;
She gave a loud screech! and I could not well blame
   her,
But lame as I was, I'd no wish to *get lamer ;*
So I made my escape—ne'er an antelope fleeter,
Lest my verse, like the poet, should limp through
   lag metre.

Dr. John Abernethy.

PALINDROMES *

PALINDROMES

ONE winter's eve around the fire, a cosy
  group, we sat,
  Engaged, as was our custom old, in after-
  dinner chat:
Small talk it was, no doubt, because the smaller
  folk were there,
And they, the young monopolists! absorbed the
  lion's share.
Conundrums, riddles, rebuses, cross-questions,
  puns atrocious,
Taxed all their ingenuity, till Peter the precocious—
Old head on shoulders juvenile—cried, 'Now for
  a new task,
Let's try our hand at Palindromes!' 'Agreed!
  But first,' we ask,
'Pray, Peter, what are Palindromes?' The forward
  imp replied,
'A Palindrome's a string of words, of sense or mean-
  ing void,
Which reads both ways the same; and here, with
  your permission,

* Words or phrases which read the same backward or forward.

[93]

I'll cite some half-a-score of samples, lacking all
    precision,
(But held together by loose rhymes) to test my
    definition!'

"A milksop jilted by his lass, or wandering in his
    wits,
Might murmur, *Stiff, O dairyman, in a myriad of
    fits !*
A limner, by photography dead beat in competition,
Thus grumbled: *No, it is opposed, art sees trade's
    opposition !*
A nonsense-loving nephew might his soldier uncle
    dun,
With *Now stop, Major-general, are negro jam pots
    won !*
A supercilious grocer, if inclined that way, might
    snub
A child with, *But Ragusa store, babe, rots a sugar
    tub !*
Thy sceptre, Alexander, is a fortress, cried Hephæs-
    tion;
Great A. said, *No, it's a bar of gold, a bad log for
    a bastion !*
A timid creature fearing rodents—mice, and such
    small fry—
Stop, Syrian, I start at rats in airy spots, might
    cry.
A simple soul, whose wants are few, might say
    with hearty zest,
*Desserts I desire not, so long no lost one rise dis-
    tressed.*

A stern Canadian parent might—in earnest, not in
   fun—
Exclaim, *No sot nor Ottawa law at Toronto, son!*
A crazy dentist might declare, as something strange
   or new,
That *Paget saw an Irish tooth, sir, in a waste-gap!*
   True!
A surly student, hating sweets, might answer with
   elan,
Name tarts, no, medieval slave, I demonstrate man!
He who in Nature's bitters findeth sweet food every
   day,
Eureka! till I pull up ill I take rue, well might say."
                                        H. Campkin.

PALINDROME LINES

SALTA, tu levis es; summus se si velut Atlas,
   (Omina se sinimus,) suminis es animo.
      Sin, oro, caret arcana cratera coronis
Unam arcas, animes semina sacra manu.
Angere regnato, mutatum, o tangere regna,
Sana tero, tauris si ruat oret anas:
Milo subi rivis, summus si viribus olim,
Muta sedes; animal lamina sede satum.
Tangeret, i videas, illisae divite regnat;
Aut atros ubinam manibus orta tua!
O tu casurus, rem non mersurus acuto
Telo, sis-ne, tenet? non tenet ensis, olet."
                                        Anonymous.

[95]

MNEMONICS

LADY MOON

(How to tell her age)

O LADY MOON, your horns point toward
    the east;
        Shine, be increased;
☾ Lady Moon, your horns point toward the west;
        Wane, be at rest.

Christina G. Rossetti.

DAYS IN THE MONTHS

THIRTY days hath September,
    April, June, and November,
        February has twenty-eight alone;
All the rest have thirty-one,
Excepting leap-year,—that's the time
When February's days are twenty-nine.

Anonymous.

THE PERFECT GREYHOUND

IF you would have a good tyke,
  Of which there are few like,—
  He must be headed like a snake,
Necked like a drake,
Backed like a bean,
Tailed like a bat,
And footed like a cat.

Old Rhyme.

THE CUCKOO

The Cuckoo's Habits

IN April,
  Come he will;
  In May,
He sings all day;
In June,
He changes his tune;
In July,
He makes ready to fly;
In August,
Go he must.

Old Rhyme.

TWO APPLE-HOWLING SONGS

[Sung in orchards by Apple-howlers on Twelfth Day.]

SURREY

HERE stands a good apple-tree.
    Stand fast at root,
      Bear well at top;
Every little twig
Bear an apple big;
Every little bough
Bear an apple now;
Hats full! Caps full!
Threescore sacks full!
Hullo, boys! hullo!

DEVONSHIRE

HERE'S to thee, old apple-tree,
    Whence thou may'st bud, and whence thou
      may'st blow,
And whence thou may'st bear apples enow!
Hats full! Caps full!
Bushel—bushel—sacks full,
Old parson's breeches full,
And my pockets full too!
    Huzza!

Anonymous.

[98]

DAYS OF BIRTH

MONDAY'S child is fair of face,
　　Tuesday's child is full of grace,
　　Wednesday's child is full of woe,
Thursday's child has far to go,
Friday's child is loving and giving,
Saturday's child works hard for its living,
And a child that's born on the Sabbath-day
Is fair and wise and good and gay.

Old Rhyme.

PROGNOSTICATIONS

CUT your nails Monday, you cut them for news;
　　Cut them on Tuesday, a pair of new shoes;
　　Cut them on Wednesday you cut them for
　　　　health;
Cut them on Thursday, 'twill add to your wealth;
Cut them on Friday, you cut them for woe;
Cut them on Saturday, a journey you'll go;
Cut them on Sunday you cut them for evil,
For all the week long you'll be ruled by the devil.

Anonymous.

HOURS OF SLEEP

NATURE requires five; custom gives seven;
Laziness takes nine, and wickedness eleven.

Anonymous.

[99]

OLD ADAGE

EARLY to bed and early to rise—
Makes a man healthy, wealthy and wise.
Anonymous.

OLD SAW

HE who would thrive, must rise at five;
He who hath thriven, may lie till seven.
Anonymous.

FRENCH ADAGE

LEVER à cinq, dîner à neuf,
Souper à cinq, coucher à neuf,
Fait vivre d'ans nonante et neuf.
Anonymous.

A CAUTION

IF you your lips
    Would keep from slips,
  Of these five things beware:
Of whom you speak,
To whom you speak,
    And how, and when, and where.
Anonymous.

CAUTIONS

HE that spendeth much,
    And getteth nought;
He that oweth much,
    And hath nought;
He that looketh in his purse
  And findeth nought—
He may be sorry,
    And say nought.

*

He that may and will not,
He then that would shall not,
He that would and cannot,
May repent and sigh not.

*

He that sweareth
  Till no man trust him;
He that lieth;
  Till no man believe him;
He that borroweth
  Till no man will lend him,—
Let him go where
  No man knoweth him.

*

He that hath a good master,
  And cannot keep him;

[101]

He that hath a good servant,
  And not content with him;
He that hath such conditions
  That no man loveth him,—
May well know other,
  But few men will know him.
                              Hugh Rhodes.

PHILOSOPHIC ADVICE

HE who knows not, and knows not that he
    knows not; he is a fool, shun him.
  He who knows not, and knows that he
    knows not; he is simple, teach him.
He who knows, and knows not that he knows;
  he is asleep, wake him.
He who knows, and knows that he knows; he is
  wise, follow him.
                              Anonymous.

THE RIGHT SORT OF A FELLOW

YOU may know the fellow
    Who thinks he thinks,
  Or the fellow who thinks he knows;
But find the fellow
    Who knows he thinks—
And you know the fellow who knows.
                              Anonymous.

A MAN OF WORDS

A MAN of words and not of deeds,
　　Is like a garden full of weeds;
　　And when the weeds begin to grow,
It's like a garden full of snow;
And when the snow begins to fall,
It's like a bird upon the wall;
And when the bird away does fly,
It's like an eagle in the sky;
And when the sky begins to roar,
It's like a lion at the door;
And when the door begins to crack,
It's like a stick across your back;
And when your back begins to smart,
It's like a penknife in your heart;
And when your heart begins to bleed,
You're dead, and dead, and dead indeed.

Anonymous.

SHERIDAN'S CALENDAR

JANUARY snowy,
　　February flowy,
　　March blowy,

April showry,
May flowery,
June bowery,

[103]

July moppy,
August croppy,
September poppy,

October breezy,
November wheezy,
December freezy.

A RULE OF THREE

THERE is a rule to drink,
        I think,
        A rule of three
That you'll agree
With me
Cannot be beaten
And tends our lives to sweeten:
Drink ere you eat,
And while you eat,
And after you have eaten!

Wallace Rice.

REASONS FOR DRINKING

IF all be true that I do think,
    There are five reasons we should drink;
    Good wine—a friend—or being dry—
Or lest we should be by and by—
Or any other reason why.

Dr. Henry Aldrich.

[104]

A BACCHANALIAN TOAST

DRINK up
    Your cup,
    But not spill wine;
    For if you
        Do
    'Tis an ill sign.

Robert Herrick.

CATALOGUE WHIMSEYS

THE HUNDRED BEST BOOKS

FIRST there's the Bible,
    And then the Koran,
    Odgers on Libel,
    Pope's Essay on Man,
Confessions of Rousseau,
    The Essays of Lamb,
Robinson Crusoe
    And Omar Khayyam,
Volumes of Shelley
    And Venerable Bede,
Machiavelli
    And Captain Mayne Reid,
Fox upon Martyrs
    And Liddell and Scott,
Stubbs on the Charters,
    The works of La Motte,
The Seasons by Thomson,
    And Paul de Verlaine,
Theodore Mommsen
    And Clemens (Mark Twain),
The Rocks of Hugh Miller,
    The Mill on the Floss,
The Poems of Schiller,
    The Iliados,

Don Quixote (Cervantes),
    La Pucelle by Voltaire,
Inferno (that's Dante's),
    And Vanity Fair,
Conybeare-Howson,
    Brillat-Savarin,
And Baron Munchausen,
    Mademoiselle De Maupin,
The Dramas of Marlowe,
    The Three Musketeers,
Clarissa Harlowe,
    And the Pioneers,
Sterne's Tristram Shandy,
    The Ring and the Book,
And Handy Andy,
    And Captain Cook,
The Plato of Jowett,
    And Mill's Pol. Econ.,
The Haunts of Howitt,
    The Encheiridion,
Lothair by Disraeli,
    And Boccaccio,
The Student's Paley,
    And Westward Ho!
The Pharmacopœia,
    Macaulay's Lays,
Of course The Medea,
    And Sheridan's Plays,
The Odes of Horace,
    And Verdant Green,
The Poems of Morris,
    The Faerie Queen,

[107]

The Stones of Venice,
　　Natural History (White's),
And then Pendennis,
　　The Arabian Nights,
Cicero's Orations,
　　Plain Tales from the Hills,
The Wealth of Nations,
　　And Byles on Bills,
As in a Glass Darkly,
　　Demosthenes' Crown,
The Treatise of Berkeley,
　　Tom Hughes's Tom Brown,
The Mahabharata,
　　The Humour of Hook,
The Kreutzer Sonata,
　　And Lalla Rookh,
Great Battles by Creasy,
　　And Hudibras,
And Midshipman Easy,
　　And Rasselas,
Shakespeare *in extenso*
　　And the Æneid,
And Euclid (Colenso),
　　The Woman who Did,
Poe's Tales of Mystery,
　　Then Rabelais,
Guizot's French History,
　　And Men of the Day,
Rienzi, by Lytton,
　　The Poems of Burns,
The Story of Britain,
　　The Journey (that's Sterne's),

[108]

The House of Seven Gables,
   Carroll's Looking-glass,
Æsop his Fables,
   And Leaves of Grass,
Departmental Ditties,
   The Woman in White,
The Tale of Two Cities,
   Ships that Pass in the Night,
Meredith's Feverel,
   Gibbon's Decline,
Walter Scott's Peveril,
   And—some verses of mine.

             Mostyn T. Pigott.

A RHYME FOR MUSICIANS

HÄNDEL, Bendel, Mendelssohn,
   Brendel, Wendel, Jadassohn,
   Müller, Hiller, Heller, Franz,
   Plothow, Flotow, Burto, Ganz.

Meyer, Geyer, Meyerbeer,
Heyer, Weyer, Beyer, Beer,
Lichner, Lachner, Schachner, Dietz,
Hill, Will, Brüll, Grill, Drill, Reiss, Rietz.

Hansen, Jansen, Jensen, Kiehl,
Siade, Gade, Laade, Stiehl,
Naumann, Riemann, Diener, Wurst,
Niemann, Kiemann, Diener, Furst.

[109]

Kochler, Dochler, Rubinstein,
Himmel, Hummel, Rosenhain,
Lauer, Bauer, Kleinecke,
Homberg, Plomberg, Reinecke.

E. Lemke.

'TIS EVER THUS

A D astra, De Profundis,
  Keats, Bacchus, Sophocles;
 Ars Longa, Euthanasia,
  Spring, The Eumenides.

Dead Leaves, Metempsychosis,
 Waiting, Theocritus;
Vanitas Vanitatum,
 My Ship, De Gustibus.

Dum Vivimus Vivamus,
 Sleep, Palingenesis;
Salvini, Sursum Corda,
 At Mt. Desert, To Miss ——.

These are part of the contents
 Of "Violets of Song,"
The first poetic volume
 Of Susan Mary Strong.

R. K. Munkittrick.

[110]

INDIAN TRIBES

THE Sioux and the Algonquins, where are
these?
    Where, too, are now the Hurons and
Pawnees,
The Chickasaws, Oneidas, and Shawnees,
The Winnebagos, and the Muscogees,
The Saukies, the Comanches, and Uchees,
The Kansas, Seminoles, and Weetumkees,
The Mohegans, Nihantics, and Natchees,
The Pequots, Miamis, and Yamasees,
The Tuscaroras and the Waterees,
The Narragansetts, and Menomonees,
The Choctaws, Delawares, and Cherokees,
The Eries, Yamacraws, and Mosokees,
The Mohawks, and the Chickahominies,
The Kickapoos, and tall Walhominies,
The Androscoggins, and the Omahas,
The Alibams, and Mitchigamuas,
The Tangeboas, and the Pammahas,
The Apalachias, and the Ostonoos,
The Sacs and Foxes and the Onodoos,
The Pottawattomies and Ioways,
The Creeks, Catawbas, and Ojibbeways,
The Senecas, Peorias, and Crows—
Who sank beneath the burden of their woes?
How few remain of all those valiant hosts
That peopled once the prairies and the coasts?
                           Anonymous

SIGNS OF RAIN

*(Forty reasons for not accepting an invitation of a
friend to make an excursion with him.)*

1. THE hollow winds begin to blow;
2. The clouds look black, the glass is low,
3. The soot falls down, the spaniels sleep,
4. And spiders from their cobwebs peep.
5. Last night the sun went pale to bed,
6. The moon in halos hid her head;
7. The boding shepherd heaves a sigh,
8. For see, a rainbow spans the sky!
9. The walls are damp, the ditches smell,
10. Closed is the pink-hued pimpernel.
11. Hark how the chairs and tables crack!
12. Old Betty's nerves are on the rack;
13. Loud quacks the duck, the peacocks cry,
14. The distant hills are seeming nigh,
15. How restless are the snorting swine!
16. The busy flies disturb the kine,
17. Low o'er the grass the swallow wings,
18. The cricket, too, how sharp he sings!
19. Puss on the hearth, with velvet paws,
20. Sits wiping o'er her whiskered jaws;
21. Through the clear streams the fishes rise,
22. And nimble catch the incautious flies.
23. The glow-worms, numerous and light,
24. Illumed the dewy dell last night;
25. At dusk the squalid toad was seen,
26. Hopping and crawling o'er the green;

27. The whirling dust the wind obeys,
28. And in the rapid eddy plays;
29. The frog has changed his yellow vest,
30. And in a russet coat is dressed.
31. Though June the air is cold and still,
32. The mellow blackbird's voice is shrill;
33. My dog, so altered in his taste,
34. Quits mutton-bones on grass to feast;
35. And see yon rooks, how odd their flight!
36. They imitate the gliding kite,
37. And seem precipitate to fall,
38. As if they felt the piercing ball.
39. 'Twill surely rain; I see with sorrow
40. Our jaunt must be put off to-morrow.

Edward Jenner.

SIMILES

As wet as a fish—as dry as a bone;
As live as a bird—as dead as a stone;
As plump as a partridge—as poor as a rat;
As strong as a horse—as weak as a cat;
As hard as a flint—as soft as a mole;
As white as a lily—as black as a coal;
As plain as a pike-staff—as rough as a bear;
As light as a drum—as free as the air;
As heavy as lead—as light as a feather;
As steady as time—uncertain as weather;
As hot as an oven—as cold as a frog;
As gay as a lark—as sick as a dog;
As slow as the tortoise—as swift as the wind;
As true as the Gospel—as false as mankind;

[113]

As thin as a herring—as fat as a pig;
As proud as a peacock—as blithe as a grig;
As savage as tigers—as mild as a dove;
As stiff as a poker—as limp as a glove;
As blind as a bat—as deaf as a post;
As cool as a cucumber—as warm as a toast;
As flat as a flounder—as round as a ball;
As blunt as a hammer—as sharp as an awl;
As red as a ferret—as safe as the stocks;
As bold as a thief—as sly as a fox;
As straight as an arrow—as crook'd as a bow;
As yellow as saffron—as black as a sloe;
As brittle as glass—as tough as gristle;
As neat as my nail—as clean as a whistle;
As good as a feast—as bad as a witch;
As light as is day—as dark as is pitch;
As brisk as a bee—as dull as an ass;
As full as a tick—as solid as brass.

Anonymous.

A NURSERY RHYME

ONE old Oxford ox opening oysters;
  Two teetotums totally tired trying to trot
   to Tadbury;
Three tall tigers tippling tenpenny tea;
Four fat friars fanning fainting flies;
Five frippy Frenchmen foolishly fishing for flies;
Six sportsmen shooting snipes;
Seven Severn salmons swallowing shrimps;
Eight Englishmen eagerly examining Europe;

Nine nimble noblemen nibbling nonpareils;
Ten tinkers tinkling upon ten tin tinder-boxes with
    ten tenpenny tacks;
Eleven elephants elegantly equipt;
Twelve typographical typographers typically trans-
    lating types.

Anonymous.

LONDON BELLS

GAY go up and gay go down,
    To ring the bells of London town.

Bull's eyes and targets,
Say the bells of St. Marg'ret's.

Brickbats and tiles,
Say the bells of St. Giles'.

Halfpence and farthings,
Say the bells of St. Martin's.

Oranges and lemons,
Say the bells of St. Clement's.

Pancakes and fritters,
Say the bells of St. Peter's.

Two sticks and an apple,
Say the bells at Whitechapel.

[115]

Old Father Baldpate,
Say the slow bells at Aldgate.

You owe me ten shillings,
Say the bells at St. Helen's.

Poker and tongs,
Say the bells at St. John's.

Kettles and pans,
Say the bells at St. Ann's.

When will you pay me?
Say the bells of Old Bailey.

When I grow rich,
Say the bells at Shoreditch.

Pray when will that be?
Say the bells at Stepney.

I am sure I don't know,
Says the great bell at Bow.

Here comes a candle to light you to bed,
And here comes a chopper to chop off your head.

Anonymous.

THE COURT OF ALDERMEN AT FISH-MONGERS' HALL

"IS that dace or perch?"
   Said Alderman Birch;
   "I take it for herring,"
  Said Alderman Perring.
"This jack's very good,"
  Said Alderman Wood;
"But its bones might a man slay,"
  Said Alderman Ansley.
"I'll butter what I get,"
  Said Alderman Heygate.
"Give me some stewed carp,"
  Said Alderman Thorp.
"The roe's dry as pith,"
  Said Alderman Smith.
"Don't cut so far down,"
  Said Alderman Brown;
"But nearer the fin,"
  Said Alderman Glyn,
"I've finished, i' faith, man,"
  Said Alderman Waithman:
"And I, too, i' fatkins,"
  Said Alderman Atkins.
"They've crimped this cod drolly,"
  Said Alderman Scholey;
"'Tis bruised at the ridges,"
  Said Alderman Brydges.
"Was it caught in a drag? Nay,"
  Said Alderman Magnay.

[117]

"'Twas brought by two men,"
    Said Alderman Ven—
ables: "Yes, in a box,"
    Said Alderman Cox.
"They care not how fur 'tis,"
    Said Alderman Curtis—
"From the air kept, and from sun,"
    Said Alderman Thompson;
"Packed neatly in straw,"
    Said Alderman Shaw:
"In ice got from Gunter,"
    Said Alderman Hunter.
"This ketchup is sour,"
    Said Alderman Flower;
"Then steep it in claret,"
    Said Alderman Garret.

Anonymous.

EARTH

WHAT is earth, Sexton?—A place to dig
    graves.
    What is earth, Rich man?—A place to
    work slaves.
What is earth, Greybeard?—A place to grow old.
What is earth, Miser?—A place to dig gold.
What is earth, Schoolboy?—A place for my play.
What is earth, Maiden?—A place to be gay.
What is earth, Seamstress?—A place where I
    weep.
What is earth, Sluggard?—A good place to sleep.

What is earth. Soldier?—A place for a battle.
What is earth, Herdsman?—A place to raise cattle.
What is earth, Widow?—A place of true sorrow.
What is earth, Tradesman?—I'll tell you to-mor-
　row.
What is earth, Sick man?—'Tis nothing to me.
What is earth, Sailor?—My home is the sea.
What is earth, Statesman?—A place to win fame.
What is earth, Author?—I'll write there my name.
What is earth, Monarch?—For my realm it is
　given.
What is earth, Christian?—The gateway of
　heaven.

Anonymous.

THE JOYS OF MARRIAGE

HOW uneasy is his life,
　　Who is troubled with a wife!
　　Be she ne'er so fair or comely,
Be she ne'er so foul or homely,
Be she ne'er so young and toward,
Be she ne'er so old and froward,
Be she kind, with arms enfolding,
Be she cross, and always scolding,
Be she blithe or melancholy,
Have she wit, or have she folly,
Be she wary, be she squandering,
Be she staid, or be she wandering,
Be she constant, be she fickle,
Be she fire, or be she ickle;

[119]

Be she pious or ungodly,
Be she chaste, or what sounds oddly:
Lastly, be she good or evil,
Be she saint, or be she devil,—
Yet, uneasy is his life
Who is married to a wife.

Charles Cotton.

A NEW-YEAR'S GIFT FOR SHREWS

WHO marrieth a wife upon a Monday,
    If she will not be good upon a Tuesday,
    Let him go to the wood upon a Wednes-
        day,
And cut him a cudgel upon the Thursday,
And pay her soundly upon a Friday:
And she mend not, the divil take her a' Saturday:
Then he may eat his meat in peace on the Sunday.

Anonymous.

ONE WEEK

THE year had gloomily begun
    For Willie Weeks, a poor man's SUN.

He was beset with bill and dun
    And he had very little MON.

"This cash," said he, "won't pay my dues,
    I've nothing here but ones and TUES."

[120]

A bright thought struck him, and he said,
      "The rich Miss Goldrocks I will WED."

But when he paid his court to her,
      She lisped, but firmly said, "No, THUR!"

"Alas!" said he, "then I must die!"
      His soul went where they say souls FRI.

They found his gloves, and coat, and hat;
      The Coroner upon them SAT.
           Carolyn Wells.

TONGUE TWISTERS

THE TWINER

WHEN a twiner a twisting will twist him a
      twist,
        For the twining his twist he three twines
            doth entwist;
But if one of the twines of the twist do untwist,
The twine that untwisteth, untwisteth the twist.

Untwirling the twine that untwisteth between,
He twists with his twister the two in a twine;
Then twice having twisted the twines of the twine,
He twisteth the twines he had twisted in vain.

The twain that, in twisting before in the twine,
As twines were entwisted, he now doth untwine,
'Twixt the twain intertwisting a twine more between
He, twisting his twister, makes a twist of the twine.

Dr. Wallis.

UN CORDIER

QUAND un cordier cordant
        Veut corder une corde,
      Trois cordons accordant
          A sa corde il accorde.

Si l'un des trois cordons
De la corde décorde,
Le cordon décordant
Fait décorder la corde.

Allain Chartier.

THE THATCHER

A THATCHER of Thatchwood went to That-
chet a-thatching;
Did a Thatcher of Thatchwood go to
Thatchet a-thatching?
If a thatcher of Thatchwood went to Thatchet a-
thatching,
Where's the thatching the thatcher of Thatchwood
has thatched?

Anonymous.

PETER PIPER

PETER PIPER picked a peck of pickled pep-
pers.
A peck of pickled peppers Peter Piper picked.
If Peter Piper picked a peck of pickled peppers,
Where's the peck of pickled peppers Peter Piper
picked?

Anonymous.

SIMPLE ENGLISH

OFTTIMES when I put on my gloves,
    I wonder if I'm sane,
      For when I put the right one on,
        The right seems to remain
To be put on—that is, 'tis left;
    Yet if the left I don,
The other one is left, and then
    I have the right one on.
But still I have the left on right;
    The right one, though, is left
To go right on the left right hand
    All right, if I am deft.

Ray Clarke Rose.

WHAT HIAWATHA PROBABLY DID

HE slew the noble Mudjekeewis,
    With his skin he made him mittens;
      Made them with the fur side inside;
Made them with the skin-side outside;
He, to keep the warm side inside,
Put the cold side, skin-side outside;
He, to keep the cold side outside,
Put the warm side, fur-side, inside:—
That's why he put the cold side outside,
Why he put the warm side inside,
Why he turned them inside outside.

Anonymous.

MONORHYMES

UNDER THE TREES

UNDER the trees!" Who but agrees
    That there is magic in words such as these?
    Promptly one sees shake in the breeze
Stately lime-avenues haunted of bees:
Where, looking far over buttercupp'd leas,
Lads and "fair shes" (that is Byron, and he's
An authority) lie very much at their ease;
Taking their teas, or their duck and green peas,
Or, if they prefer it, their plain bread and cheese:
Not objecting at all, though it's rather a squeeze,
And the glass is, I daresay, at 80 degrees.
Some get up glees, and are mad about Ries
And Sainton, and Tamberlik's thrilling high Cs;
Or if painters, hold forth upon Hunt and Maclise,
And the tone and the breadth of that landscape of
    Lee's;
Or, if learned, on nodes and the moon's apogees,
Or, if serious, on something of A.K.H.B.'s,
Or the latest attempt to convert the Chaldees;
Or in short about all things, from earthquakes to
    fleas.
Some sit in twos or (less frequently) threes,
With their innocent lambswool or book on their
    knees,

[125]

And talk, and enact, any nonsense you please,
As they gaze into eyes that are blue as the seas;
And you hear an occasional "Harry, don't tease"
From the sweetest of lips in the softest of keys,
And other remarks, which to me are Chinese.
And fast the time flees; till a ladylike sneeze,
Or a portly papa's more elaborate wheeze,
Makes Miss Tabitha seize on her brown muffatees,
And announce as a fact that it's going to freeze,
And that young people ought to attend to their Ps
And their Qs, and not court every form of disease.
Then Tommy eats up the three last ratafias,
And pretty Louise wraps her *robe de cerise*
Round a bosom as tender as Widow Machree's,
And (in spite of the pleas of her lorn *vis-a-vis*)
Goes to wrap up her uncle—a patient of Skey's,
Who is prone to catch chills, like all old Bengalese:—
But at bedtime I trust he'll remember to grease
The bridge of his nose, and preserve his rupees
From the premature clutch of his fond legatees;
Or at least have no fees to pay any M.D.s
For the cold his niece caught, sitting under the Trees.

C. S. Calverley.

THE RULING POWER

GOLD! Gold! Gold! Gold!
    Bright and yellow, hard and cold,
       Molten, graven, hammered and rolled;
Heavy to get, and light to hold;
Hoarded, bartered, bought and sold,

Stolen, borrowed, squandered, doled;
Spurned by the young, but hugged by the old,
To the very verge of the churchyard mould;
Price of many a crime untold;
Gold! Gold! Gold! Gold!
Good or bad, a thousandfold!

Thomas Hood

THE MUSICAL ASS

THE fable which I now present,
   Occurred to me by accident:
   And whether bad or excellent,
Is merely so by accident.

A stupid ass this morning went
Into a field by accident:
And cropped his food, and was content,
Until he spied by accident
A flute, which some oblivious gent
Had left behind by accident;
When, sniffling it with eager scent,
He breathed on it by accident,
And made the hollow instrument
Emit a sound by accident.
" Hurrah, hurrah!" exclaimed the brute,
" How cleverly I play the flute!"

A fool, in spite of nature's bent,
May shine for once,—by accident.

Tomaso de Yriarte

THE ROMAN NOSE

THAT Roman nose! that Roman nose!
  Has robbed my bosom of repose;
  For when in sleep my eyelids close,
  It haunts me still, that Roman nose!

Between two eyes as black as sloes
The bright and flaming ruby glows:
That Roman nose! that Roman nose!
And beats the blush of damask rose.

I walk the streets, the alleys, rows;
I look at all the Jems and Joes;
And old and young, and friends and foes,
But cannot find a Roman nose!

Then blessed be the day I chose
That nasal beauty of my beau's;
And when at last to Heaven I goes,
I hope to spy his Roman nose!

Merrie England

TO MRS. THRALE ON HER THIRTY-FIFTH BIRTHDAY

OFT in danger, yet alive,
  We are come to thirty-five;
  Long may better years arrive,
Better years than thirty-five.

Could philosophers contrive
Life to stop at thirty-five,
Time his hours should never drive
O'er the bounds of thirty-five.
High to soar, and deep to dive,
Nature gives at thirty-five.
Ladies, stock and tend your hive,
Trifle not at thirty-five;
For, howe'er we boast and strive,
Life declines from thirty-five.
He that ever hopes to thrive
Must begin by thirty-five;
And all who wisely wish to wive
Must look on Thrale at thirty-five.

Boswell.

A RHYME FOR TIPPERARY

A POET there was in sad quandary,
    To find a rhyme for Tipperary.
    Long laboured he through January,
Yet found no rhyme for Tipperary;
Toiled every day in February,
But toiled in vain for Tipperary;
Searched Hebrew text and commentary
But searched in vain for Tipperary;
Bored all his friends in Inverary,
To find a rhyme for Tipperary;
Implored the aid of "Paddy Cary,"
Yet still no rhyme for Tipperary;
He next besought his mother Mary
To tell him rhyme for Tipperary;

[129]

But she, good woman, was no fairy,
Nor witch,—though born in Tipperary;
Knew everything about her dairy,
But not the rhyme for Tipperary;
The stubborn Muse he could not vary,
For still the lines would run contrary
Whene'er he thought on Tipperary.
And though of time he was not chary,
'Twas thrown away on Tipperary.
Till of his wild-goose chase most weary,
He vowed he'd leave out Tipperary.
But no—the theme he might not vary,
His longing was not temporary,
To find meet rhyme for Tipperary.
He sought among the gay and airy,
He pestered all the military.
Committed many a strange vagary,
Bewitched, it seemed, by Tipperary.
He wrote, post-haste, to Darby Leary,
Besought with tears his Aunty Sairie;
But sought he far, or sought he near, he
Ne'er found a rhyme for Tipperary.
He travelled sad through Cork and Kerry,
He drove like mad through sweet Dunleary,
Kicked up a precious tantar-ara,
But found no rhyme for Tipperary;
Lived fourteen weeks at Stan-ar-ara,
Was well-nigh lost in Glenegary,
Then started slick for Denerara,
In search of rhyme for Tipperary.
Through Yankee-land, sick, solitary.
He roamed by forest, lake, and prairie,

[130]

He went *per terram et per mare*,
But found no rhyme for Tipperary.
Through orient climes on Dromedary,
On camel's back through great Sahara;
His travels were extraordinary
In search of rhyme for Tipperary.
Fierce as a gorgon on chimæra,
Fierce as Alecto or Megaera,
Fiercer than e'er a love-sick bear, he
Ranged through the "londe" of Tipperary.
His cheeks grew thin and wondrous hairy,
His visage long, his aspect "eerie,"
His *tout ensemble*, faith, would scare ye,
Amidst the wilds of Tipperary.
Becoming hypochon-dri-ary,
He sent for his apothecary,
Who ordered "balm" and "saponary,"
Herbs rare to find in Tipperary.
In his potations ever wary,
His choicest drink was "home gooseberry."
On swipes, skim-milk, and smallest beer, he
Hunted rhyme for his Tipperary.
Had he imbibed good old Madeira,
Drank pottle-deep of golden sherry
Of Falstaff's sack, or ripe Canary,
No rhyme had lacked for Tipperary
Or had his tastes been literary,
He might have found extemporary
Without the aid of dictionary,
Some fitting rhyme for Tipperary.
Or had he seen an antiquary,
Burnt midnight oil in his library,

Or been of temper less "camstary,"
Rhymes had not lacked for Tipperary.
He paced about his aviary,
Blew up, sky-high, his secretary,
And then in wrath and anger sware he,
There was *no* rhyme for Tipperary.

Dr. Fitzgerald.

THE DONERAILE LITANY

ALAS! how dismal is my tale!—
I lost my watch in Doneraile;
My Dublin watch, my chain and seal,
Pilfered at once in Doneraile.

May fire and brimstone never fail
To fall in showers on Doneraile;
May all the leading fiends assail
The thieving town of Doneraile.

As lightnings flash across the vale,
So down to hell with Doneraile;
The fate of Pompey at Pharsale,
Be that the curse of Doneraile.

May beef or mutton, lamb or veal,
Be never found in Doneraile;
But garlic-soup and scurvy kail
Be still the food for Doneraile.

And forward as the creeping snail
The industry be of Doneraile;
May Heaven a chosen curse entail
On rigid, rotten Doneraile.

May sun and moon for ever fail
To beam their lights in Doneraile;
May every pestilential gale
Blast that curst spot called Doneraile.

May no sweet cuckoo, thrush, or quail,
Be ever heard in Doneraile;
May patriots, kings, and commonweal,
Despise and harass Doneraile.

May every Post, Gazette, and Mail,
Sad tidings bring of Doneraile;
May loudest thunders ring a peal
To blind and deafen Doneraile.

May vengeance fall at head and tail,
From north to south, at Doneraile;
May profit light, and tardy sale,
Still damp the trade of Doneraile.

May Fame resound a dismal tale,
Whene'er she lights on Doneraile;
May Egypt's plagues at once prevail,
To thin the knaves of Doneraile.

May frost and snow, and sleet and hail,
Benumb each joint in Doneraile;

May wolves and bloodhounds trace and trail
The cursed crew of Doneraile.

May Oscar, with his fiery flail,
To atoms thresh all Doneraile;
May every mischief, fresh and stale,
Abide henceforth in Doneraile.

May all, from Belfast to Kinsale,
Scoff, curse, and damn you, Doneraile;
May neither flour nor oatenmeal
Be found or known in Doneraile.

May want and woe each joy curtail
That e'er was known in Doneraile;
May no one coffin want a nail
That wraps a rogue in Doneraile.

May all the thieves that rob and steal
The gallows meet in Doneraile;
May all the sons of Granaweal
Blush at the thieves of Doneraile.

May mischief, big as Norway whale,
O'erwhelm the knaves of Doneraile;
May curses, wholesale and retail,
Pour with full force on Doneraile.

May every transport wont to sail,
A convict bring from Doneraile;
May every churn and milking-pail
Fall dry to staves in Doneraile.

[134]

May cold and hunger still congeal
The stagnant blood of Doneraile;
May every hour new woes reveal
That hell reserves for Doneraile.

May every chosen ill prevail
O'er all the imps of Doneraile;
May no one wish or prayer avail
To soothe the woes of Doneraile.

May the Inquisition straight impale
The rapparees of Doneraile;
May Charon's boat triumphant sail,
Completely manned, from Doneraile.

Oh, may my couplets never fail
To find a curse for Doneraile;
And may grim Pluto's inner jail
For ever groan with Doneraile.

Patrick O'Kelly.

MY MANX MINX

ALL the Bard's rhymes, and all his inks,
   Will scarce pourtray the Proteus—MINX:

Nor artist brush with brightest tincts
Of Fancy's rainbow picture MINX.

The child of Man and beast: a sphinx
Of noble rearing: that is MINX.

[135]

With paw of leopard, eye of lynx,
And spring of tiger, such is MINX.

She's playful, harmless: Mousie thinks:
But dreadful earnest's artful MINX.

Seems nonchalante, and bobs, and blinks:
Ma foi, toute autre chose is MINX.

Formitat Homer oft: her winks
Are rare: no "nid-nid-niddin"—MINX.

Aye "takkin notes" of holes and chinks:
A slee and pawky body's MINX.

An Abbess of Misrule: she slinks
From no malfeasance: wilful MINX.

(Law:)—Ne quid nim, of neighbour's trinks:
She's always nimming: roguish MINX.

With reels of silk, thread, wool, plays rinks:
Tossing and tangling: tricksy MINX.

Loves, frisks, curvets, and highest jinks:
Frolic's own daughter, merry MINX.

As high-born dame in idlesse sinks,
So idleth fa-niente MINX.

A pert, coquettish, flirting finks:
Has fifty beaux at once: vain MINX.

Simplex munditiis, all sminks
And smears of sluthood shun spruce MINX.

Soprani trill their tink-a-tinks:
My prima-cat-atrice's MINX.

Horns blare, drums beat, and cymbal clinks:
No mewsic equals mews of MINX.

His richest creams, nectareous drinks,
Her master sets aside for MINX.

From human cares and snares he shrinks,
To spend serener hours with MINX.

The Dean's rare taste in his precincts
Pets wild ducks: I pet wilder MINX.

Of the Cat world the pink of pinks
Is tailless, peerless, *schönste* MINX.

'*Es àeí* twinned, the Bard enlinks
The names for ever: OTHO, MINX.
                    Orlando Thomas Dobbin.

FIVE WINES

B RISK methinks I am, and fine
     When I drink my cap'ring wine;
     Then to love I do incline,
When I drink my wanton wine;

And I wish all maidens mine,
When I drink my sprightly wine;
Well I sup and well I dine,
When I drink my frolic wine;
But I languish, lower, and pine,
When I want my fragrant wine.

Robert Herrick.

LINES ON ROSE *

(Written by One Who Was Restricted as to Terminals)

I. ON HER DOMESTICITY

" AS pants the heart that is the roe's,"
    So sings sweet Rosalie a lied;
Or in her pretty garden hoes,
    Or pipes soft music on a reed.

II. ON HER VANITY

She trips across the lawn, fair Rose,
    Eyes follow where her footsteps lead,
And catch a glimpse of scarlet hose,
    (She knows that he who runs may read).

* By permission of Harper & Brothers.

[138]

III. On Her Adaptability

To heaven's heights, the fierce flames rose,
   Stone, iron, melted, just like lead;
Right hard they worked with pump and hose,
   All night by flames her book she read.

IV. On Her Femininity

She planted peas, but not in rows,
   Just where her errant fancy led;
I laughed at her with loud "ho, ho's"
   Until she blushed a rosy red.

Charles Battell Loomis.

INTERIOR RHMYES

BOWLED

WHEN I, sir, play at cricket, sick it makes
        me feel;
    For I the wicket kick it backward with
        my heel.
Then, oh! such rollers bowlers always give to me,
And the rounders, grounders, too, rise and strike
    my knee;
When I in anguish languish, try to force a smile,
While laughing critics round me sound me on my
    style.

Anonymous.

A NOCTURNAL SKETCH

EVEN is come; and from the dark Park, hark,
    The signal of the setting sun—one gun!
    And six is sounding from the chime, prime
      time
To go and see the Drury-Lane Dane slain,—
Or hear Othello's jealous doubt spout out,—
Or Macbeth raving at that shade-made blade,

[140]

Denying to his frantic clutch much touch;—
Or else to see Ducrow with wide stride ride
Four horses as no other man can span;
Or in the small Olympic Pit, sit split
Laughing at Liston, while you quiz his phiz.
Anon Night comes, and with her wings brings things
Such as, with his poetic tongue, Young sung;
The gas up-blazes with its bright white light,
And paralytic watchmen prowl, howl, growl,
About the streets and take up Pall-Mall Sal,
Who, hasting to her nightly jobs, robs fobs.

Now thieves to enter for your cash, smash, crash,
Past drowsy Charley, in a deep sleep, creep,
But frightened by Policeman B 3, flee,
And while they're going, whisper low, "No go!"
Now puss, while folks are in their beds, treads leads.
And sleepers waking, grumble—"Drat that cat!"
Who in the gutter caterwauls, squalls, mauls
Some feline foe, and screams in shrill ill-will.

Now Bulls of Bashan, of a prize size, rise
In childish dreams, and with a roar gore poor
Georgy, or Charley, or Billy, willy-nilly;—
But Nursemaid, in a nightmare rest, chest-pressed,
Dreameth of one of her old flames, James Games,
And that she hears—what faith is man's!—Ann's
    banns
And his, from Reverend Mr. Rice, twice, thrice:
White ribbons flourish, and a stout shout out,
That upward goes, shows Rose knows those bows'
    woes!

                     Thomas Hood.

THE DOUBLE KNOCK

(Initial Rhymes)

R AT-TAT it went upon the lion's chin;
    "That hat, I know it!" cried the joyful girl;
    "Summer's it is, I know him by his knock;
Comers like him are welcome as the day!
Lizzy! go down and open the street-door;
Busy I am to any one but him.
Know him you must—he has been often here;
Show him upstairs, and tell him I'm alone."

Quickly the maid went tripping down the stair;
Thickly the heart of Rose Matilda beat;
"Sure he has brought me tickets for the play—
Drury—or Covent Garden—darling man!
Kemble will play—or Kean, who makes the soul
Tremble in Richard or the frenzied Moor—
Farren, the stay and prop of many a farce
Barren beside—or Liston, Laughter's Child—
Kelly the natural, to witness whom
Jelly is nothing to the public's jam—
Cooper, the sensible—and Walter Knowles
Super, in William Tell, now rightly told.
Better—perchance, from Andrews, brings a box,
Letter of boxes for the Italian stage—
Brocard! Donzelli! Taglioni! Paul!
No card,—thank Heaven—engages me to-night!
Feathers, of course—no turban, and no toque—
Weather's against it, but I'll go in curls.

[142]

Dearly I dote on white—my satin dress,
Merely one night—it won't be much the worse—
Cupid—the new *ballet* I long to see—
Stupid! why don't she go and ope the door!"

Glistened her eye as the impatient girl
Listened, low bending o'er the topmost stair,
Vainly, alas! she listens and she bends,
Plainly she hears this question and reply:
"Axes your pardon, sir, but what d'ye want?"
"Taxes," says he, "and shall not call again!"
                                    Thomas Hood.

THE FUTURE OF THE CLASSICS

NO longer, O scholars, shall Plautus
            Be taught us.
    No more shall professors be partial
            To Martial.
            No ninny
        Will stop playing "shinney"
            For Pliny.
Not even the veriest Mexican Greaser
        Will stop to read Cæsar.
No true son of Erin will leave his potato
To list to the love-lore of Ovid or Plato.
        Old Homer,
    That hapless old roamer,
Will ne'er find a rest 'neath collegiate dome or
        Anywhere else.   As to Seneca,

Any cur
Safely may snub him, or urge ill
Effects from the reading of Virgil.
Cornelius Nepos
Wont keep us
Much longer from pleasure's light errands—
Nor Terence.
The irreverent now may all scoff in ease
At the shade of poor old Aristophanes.
And moderns it now doth behoove in all
Ways to despise poor old Juvenal;
And to chivvy
Livy.
The class-room hereafter will miss a row
Of eager young students of Cicero.
The 'longshoreman—yes, and the dock-rat, he's
Down upon Socrates.
And what'll
Induce us to read Aristotle?
We shall fail in
Our duty to Galen.
No tutor henceforward shall rack us
To construe old Horatius Flaccus.
We have but a wretched opinion
Of Mr. Justinian.
In our classical pabulum mix we've no wee sop
Of Æsop.
Our balance of intellect asks for no ballast
From Sallust.
With feminine scorn no fair Vassar-bred lass at
us
Shall smile if we own that we cannot read Tacitus.

[144]

No admirer shall ever now wreathe with begonias
The bust of Suetonius.
And so, if you follow me,
We'll have to cut Ptolemy.
Besides, it would just be considered facetious
To look at Lucretius.
And you can
Not go in Society if you read Lucan,
And we cannot have any fun
Out of Xenophon.

Anonymous.

JOCOSA LYRA

IN our hearts is the Great One of Avon
Engraven,
And we climb the cold summits once built on
By Milton.

But at times not the air that is rarest
Is fairest,
And we long in the valley to follow
Apollo.

Then we drop from the heights atmospheric
To Herrick,
Or we pour the Greek honey, grown blander,
Of Landor;

Or our cosiest nook in the shade is
Where Praed is,

[145]

Or we toss the light bells of the mocker
　　　　　　With Locker.

Oh, the song where not one of the Graces
　　　　　　Tight-laces,—
Where we woo the sweet Muses not starchly,
　　　　　　But archly,—

Where the verse, like a piper a-Maying,
　　　　　　Comes playing,—
And the rhyme is as gay as a dancer
　　　　　　In answer,—

It will last till men weary of pleasure
　　　　　　In measure!
It will last till men weary of laughter . . .
　　　　　　And after!
　　　　　　　　　　Austin Dobson.

A TRIP TO PARIS

WHEN a man travels he mustn't look queer
　　If he gets a few rubs that he doesn't get
　　　　here;
And if he to Paris from Calais will stray,
I will tell him some things he will meet on his way.
Dover heights—men like mites—skiffery, cliffery,
　　Shakespeare.
Can't touch prog—sick as a dog—packet 'em,
　　racket 'em, makes pier.

[146]

Calais clerks — custom-house sharks — lurchery,
    searchery, fee! fee!
On the pavé—cabriolet—clattery, pattery, oui! oui!
Abbéville—off goes a wheel—hammery, dammery,
    tut! tut!
Montreuil—look like a fool—latery, gatery, shut!
    shut!
Laughing, quaffing, snoozing, boozing, cantering,
    bantering, gad about, mad about—
                    When a man travels, etc.

Ding dong—postboy's thong—smackery, crack-
    ery, gar! gar!
Soups, ragouts—messes and stews—hashery, trash-
    ery, psha! psha!
Beggar's woes—donnes quelque chose—howlery,
    growlery, sou! sou!
Crawl like a calf—post and a half—sluggery, tug-
    gery, pooh! pooh!
Saint-Denis — custom-house fee — lacery, tracery,
    non, non!
Silver-tip—ginger on lip—feeing 'em, freeing 'em,
    bon, bon!
                    Laughing, quaffing, etc.

When a man travels, and gets by good luck
To Paris, he stares like a pig that is stuck;
And, if he's in want of a Guide de Paris,
He'd better be quiet and listen to me.
Montagne Russe—down like a sluice—whizzery,
    dizzery, see-saw!
Catacombs—ghosts and gnomes—bonery, groan-
    ery, fee faw!

[147]

Mille Colonnes—queen on her throne—flattery,
  chattery, charmant!
Who's to pay?—Beauvilliers—suttle 'em, guttle
  'em, gourmand!
Saint-Cloud—fête of St.-Leu—bower 'em, shower
  'em, jet d'eau.
Bastille—water-work wheel—Elephant, elephant,
  wet oh!
                    Laughing, quaffing, etc.

Sol fa—Tanta-ra-ra! Shriekery, squeakery, strum,
  strum,
Louis d'or—couldn't get more—packery, backery,
  glum, glum!
Call for a bill—worse than a pill—largery, charg-
  ery, oh! oh!
Diligence—lessens expense—waggon 'em, drag-
  gin' 'em, slow, slow!
Quillacq—glad to get back—floodery, scuddery,
  sick, sick!
Now we steer—right for the pier—over 'em, Dover
  'em, quick, quick!
Laughing, quaffing, snoozing, boozing, cantering,
  bantering, gad about, mad about—
When a man travels he mustn't look queer
If he gets a few rubs that he doesn't get here;
And if he from Calais to Paris would stray,
I've told him the things he will meet on his way.
                                      James Smith.

A FERRY TALE *

O COME and cross over to nowhere,
    And go where
The nobodies live on their nothing a day!
A tideful of tricks in this merry
    Old Ferry,
And these are things that it does by the way:

It pours into parks and disperses
    The nurses;
It goes into gardens and scatters the cats;
It leaks into lodgings, disorders
    The borders,
And washes away with their holiday hats.

It soaks into shops, and inspires
    The buyers
To crawl over counters and climb upon chairs;
It trickles on tailors, it spatters
    On hatters,
And makes little milliners scamper up-stairs.

It goes out of town and it rambles
    Through brambles;
It wallows in hollows and dives into dells;
It flows into farmyards and sickens
    The chickens,
And washes the wheelbarrows into the wells.

* By permission of the Century Company.

[149]

It turns into taverns and drenches
> The benches;
It jumps into pumps and comes out with a roar;
It sounds like a postman at lodges—
> Then dodges
And runs up the lane when they open the door.

It leaks into laundries and wrangles
> With mangles;
It trips over turnips and tumbles down-hill;
It rolls like a coach along highways
> And byways,
But never gets anywhere, go as it will!

Oh, foolish old Ferry! all muddles
> And puddles—
Go fribble and dribble along on your way;
We drink to your health with molasses
> In glasses,
And waft you farewell with a handful of hay!
> *Charles E. Carryl.*

SONG FOR A CRACKED VOICE

WHEN I was young and slender, a spender,
> a lender,
> What gentleman adventurer was prankier
> than I,
Who lustier at passes with glasses—and lasses,
> How pleasant was the look of 'em as I came
> jaunting by!

(But now there's none to sigh at me as I come
creaking by.)

Then Pegasus went loping 'twixt hoping and toping,
A song in every dicky-bird, a scent in every rose;
What moons for lovelorn glances, romances, and
dances,
And how the spirit of the waltz went thrilling to
my toes!
(Egad, it's now a gouty pang goes thrilling to my
toes!)

Was I that lover frantic, romantic, and antic
Who found the lute in Molly's voice, the heaven in
her eyes,
Who, madder than a hatter, talked patter? No
matter.
Call not that little, youthful ghost, but leave it
where it lies!
(Dear, dear, how many winter snows have drifted
where she lies!)

But now I'm old and humble, why mumble and
grumble
At all the posy-linked rout that hurries laughing
by?
Framed in my gold-rimmed glasses each lass is who
passes,
And Youth is still a-twinkling in the corner of
my eye.
(How strange you cannot see it in the corner of
my eye!)

Wallace Irwin.

[151]

BLANK VERSE IN PROSE *

DEATH OF LITTLE NELL

A ND now the bell—the bell
    She had so often heard by night and day
    And listened to with solemn pleasure,
        E'en as a living voice—
Rang its remorseless toll for her,
So young, so beautiful, so good.

      Decrepit age, and vigorous life,
And blooming youth, and helpless infancy,
Poured forth—on crutches, in the pride of strength
      And health, in the full blush
Of promise—the mere dawn of life—
To gather round her tomb. Old men were there
      Whose eyes were dim
      And senses failing—
Granddames, who might have died ten years ago,
And still been old—the deaf, the blind, the lame,
      The palsied,
The living dead in many shapes and forms,
To see the closing of this early grave!
      What was the death it would shut in,
To that which still would crawl and creep above it!

* These specimens of rhythmical prose are copied verbatim from the books in which they appear.

Along the crowded path they bore her now;
    Pure as the new fallen snow
That covered it; whose day on earth
    Had been as fleeting.
Under that porch where she had sat when Heaven
In mercy brought her to that peaceful spot,
    She passed again, and the old church
    Received her in its quiet shade.

    Oh! it is hard to take
The lesson that such deaths will teach,
    But let no man reject it,
  For it is one that all must learn
  And is a mighty universal Truth.
When Death strikes down the innocent and young,
From every fragile form from which he lets
    The panting spirit free,
    A hundred virtues rise,
In shapes of mercy, charity, and love,
  To walk the world and bless it.
    Of every tear
That sorrowing mortals shed on such green graves,
Some good is born, some gentler nature comes.
          Charles Dickens
        (*in "Old Curiosity Shop"*).

SONG OF THE KETTLE

IT'S a dark night, sang the kettle, and the
   rotten leaves are lying by the way;
   And above, all is mist and darkness, and
      below, all is mire and clay;
And there is only one relief in all the sad and murky
   air,
And I don't know that it is one, for it's nothing but
   a glare
Of deep and angry crimson, where the sun and
   wind together
Set a brand upon the clouds for being guilty of
   such weather;
And the widest open country is a long dull streak
   of black;
And there's hoarfrost on the finger-post, and thaw
   upon the track;
And the ice it isn't water, and the water isn't free;
And you couldn't say that anything was what it
   ought to be;
But he's coming, coming, coming!—
                         Charles Dickens
             (*in "The Cricket on the Hearth"*).

FIXED FORMS

VILLANELLE

IT'S all a trick, quite easy when you know it
    As easy as reciting A, B, C.
    You need not be an atom of a poet.

If you've a grain of wit and want to show it,
    Writing a Villanelle—take this from me—
It's all a trick, quite easy when you know it.

You start a pair of "rimes" and then you "go it,"
    With rapid running pen and fancy free,
You need not be an atom of a poet.

Take any thought, write round it or below it,
    Above or near it, as it liketh thee;
It's all a trick, quite easy when you know it.

Pursue your task, till, like a shrub, you grow it,
    Up to the standard size it ought to be;
You need not be an atom of a poet.

Clear it of weeds, and water it, and hoe it,
    Then watch it blossom with triumphant glee,
It's all a trick, quite easy when you know it.
You need not be an atom of a poet.

                                    Walter W. Sleat.

THE RONDEAU

YOU bid me try, Blue-eyes, to write
    A Rondeau.   What! forthwith?—to-night?
      Reflect?   Some skill I have, 'tis true;
    But thirteen lines!—and rhymed on two!—
"Refrain," as well.   Ah, hapless plight!
Still there are five lines—ranged aright.
These Gallic bonds, I feared, would fright
    My easy Muse.   They did, till you—
              You bid me try!

That makes them eight.—The port's in sight;
'Tis all because your eyes are bright!
    Now just a pair to end in "oo,"—
    When maids command, what can't we do?
Behold!   The Rondeau—tasteful, light—
              You bid me try!
                  Austin Dobson.

THE ROUNDEL

A ROUNDEL is wrought as a ring or a star-
    bright sphere.
    With craft of delight and with cunning of
      sound unsought,
    That the heart of the hearer may smile if
      to pleasure his ear
      A roundel is wrought.

[156]

Its jewel of music is carven of all or of aught—
Love, laughter, or mourning—remembrance of rap-
    ture or fear—
That fancy may fashion to hang in the ear of
    thought.

As a bird's quick song runs round, and the hearts
    in us hear
Pause answer to pause, and again the same strain
    caught,
So moves the device whence, round as a pearl or
    tear,
        A roundel is wrought.
                            A. C. Swinburne.

VILLANELLE OF THINGS AMUSING

THESE are the things that make me laugh—
        Life's a preposterous farce, say I!
        And I've missed of too many jokes by half.

The high-heeled antics of colt and calf,
    The men who think they can act, and try—
These are the things that make me laugh.

The hard-boiled poses in photograph,
    The groom still wearing his wedding tie—
And I've missed of too many jokes by half!

These are the bubbles I gayly quaff
    With the rank conceit of the new-born fly—
These are the things that make me laugh!

[157]

For, Heaven help me! I needs must chaff,
   And people will tickle me till I die—
And I've missed of too many jokes, by half!

So write me down in my epitaph
As one too fond of his health to cry—
These are the things that make me laugh,
And I've missed of too many jokes by half!
                    Gelett Burgess.

TEMA CON VARIAZIONI *

I NEVER *loved a dear gazelle*—
     Nor anything that cost me much:
  High prices profit those who sell,
     But why should I be fond of such?

To glad me with his soft black eye
  My son comes trotting home from school:
He's had a fight, but can't tell why—
  He always was a little fool!

But, when he came to know me well,
  He kicked me out, her testy Sire;
And when I stained my hair, that Belle
  Might note the change, and thus admire

* By permission of the Macmillan Company.

[158]

And love me, it was sure to dye
 A muddy green or staring blue:
While one might trace, with half an eye,
 The still-triumphant carrot through.
                              Lewis Carroll.

THE TRIOLET

EASY is the triolet,
    If you really learn to make it!
   Once a neat refrain you get,
    Easy is the triolet.
As you see!—I pay my debt
 With another rhyme. Deuce take it,
Easy is the triolet,
 If you really learn to make it!
                              W. E. Henley.

TRIOLET

I LOVE you, my lord!"
    Was all that she said—
    What a dissonant chord,
 "I love you, my lord!"
Ah! how I abhorred
 That sarcastic maid!—
"*I* love you? My *Lord!*"
 Was all that she said.
                              Paul T. Gilbert.

[159]

A PITCHER OF MIGNONETTE

(*Triolet*)

A PITCHER of mignonette,
    In a tenement's highest casement:
    Queer sort of flower-pot—yet
That pitcher of mignonette
Is a garden in heaven set,
  To the little sick child in the basement—
The pitcher of mignonette,
  In the tenement's highest casement.

H. C. Bunner

THE TRIOLET

I INTENDED an Ode,
    And it turned into Triolets.
  It began à la mode:
I intended an Ode,
But Rose crossed the road
  With a bunch of fresh violets.
I intended an Ode,
  And it turned into Triolets.

I intended an Ode,
  And it turned out a Sonnet,
It began à la mode,
I intended an Ode;

But Rose crossed the road
    In her latest new bonnet.
I intended an Ode,
    And it turned out a Sonnet.
                    Austin Dobson.

BALLADE

I OFTEN does a quiet read
    At Booty Shelly's poetry;
I think that Swinburne at a screed
    Is really almost too-too fly;
At Signor Vagna's harmony
  I likes a merry little flutter;
I've had at Pater many a shy;
    In fact my form's the Bloomin' Utter.

My mark's a tiny little feed,
    And Enery Irving's gallery,
To see old 'Amlick do a bleed,
    And Ellen Terry on the die,
    Or Franky's ghostes at hi-spy,
And parties carried on a shutter.
  Them vulgar Coupeaus is my eye!
In fact my form's the Bloomin' Utter.

The Grosvenor's nuts—it is, indeed!
    I goes for 'Olman 'Unt like pie.
It's equal to a friendly lead
    To see B. Jones's judes go by.

Stanhope he makes me fit to cry,
Whistler he makes me melt like butter,
    Strudwick he makes me flash my cly,
In fact my form's the Bloomin' Utter.

Envoy.

I'm on for any Art that's 'Igh;
I talks as quite as I can splutter;
    I keeps a Dado on the sly;
In fact my form's the Bloomin' Utter!
                                W. E. Henley.

VILLANELLE

NOW ain't they utterly too-too
        (She ses, my Missus mine, ses she)
    Them flymy little bits of Blue.

Joe, just you kool 'em—nice and skew
    Upon our old meogginee,
Now ain't they utterly too-too?

They're better than a pot'n' a screw,
    They're equal to a Sunday spree,
Them flymy little bits of Blue!

Suppose I put 'em up the flue,
    And booze the profits, Joe? Not me.
Now ain't they utterly too-too?

I do the 'Igh Art fake, I do.
   Joe, I'm consummate; and I *see*
Them flymy little bits of Blue.

Which, Joe, is why I ses to you—
   Æsthetic-like, and limp, and free—
Now *ain't* they utterly too-too,
Them flymy little bits of Blue?
                  W. E. Henley.

A RONDELAY

MAN is for woman made,
    And woman made for man:
   As the spur is for the jade,
As the scabbard for the blade,
  As for liquor is the can,
So man's for woman made,
   And woman made for man.

As the sceptre to be sway'd,
As to night the serenade,
  As for pudding is the pan,
  As to cool us is the fan,
So man's for woman made,
   And woman made for man.

Be she widow, wife, or maid,
Be she wanton, be she staid,
Be she well or ill array'd,
So man's for woman made,
   And woman made for man.
              Peter A. Motteux.

[163]

SONNET TO ORDER

A SONNET would you have? Know you, my
pet,
    For sonnets fourteen lines are necessary.
    Ah, necessary rhymes, by luck to fairy—
I'll call you one, and the first quatrain get.
This meets half-way the second; half-way met.
    One meets an obstacle in a manner airy.
    But here, though it is not your name, as Mary
I'll set you down, settling the second set.

Now, you'll admit, a sonnet without love,
    Without the savour of a woman in't,
    Were profanation of poetic art.
Love, above all things! So 'tis writ above.
    Nor there alone. Your sonneteer, I'd hint,
    Gives you this sonnet here with all his heart.
                Henry Cuyler Bunner.

SONNET ON THE SONNET

TO write a sonnet doth my Julia press me;
    I've never found me in such stress or pain;
    A sonnet numbers fourteen lines, 'tis plain,
And three are gone ere I can say, God bless me!

I thought that spinning lines would sore oppress me,
    Yet here I'm midway in the last quatrain:
    And if the foremost tercet I begin,
The quatrains need not any more distress me.

[164]

To the first tercet I have got at last,
  And travel through it with such right good will,
That with this line I've finished it, I ween:

I'm in the second now, and see how fast
  The thirteenth line comes tripping from my quill:
Hurrah! 'tis done! Count if there be fourteen.
James Y. Gibson.

SONNET TO A CLAM

(Dum tacent clamant)

INGLORIOUS friend! most confident I am
  Thy life is one of very little ease;
  Albeit men mock thee with their similes
And prate of being "happy as a clam!"
What though thy shell protects thy fragile head
  From the sharp bailiffs of the briny sea?
  Thy valves are, sure, no safety-valves to thee,
While rakes are free to desecrate thy bed,
And bear thee off—as foemen take their spoil—
  Far from thy friends and family to roam;
  Forced, like a Hessian, from thy native home,
To meet destruction in a foreign broil!
  Though thou art tender yet thy humble bard
  Declares, O clam! thy case is shocking hard!
John G. Saxe.

RONDEAU

JENNY kissed me when we met,
    Jumping from the chair she sat in;
    Time, you thief, who love to get
    Sweets into your list, put that in;
Say I'm weary, say I'm sad,
    Say that health and wealth have missed me,
Say I'm growing old, but add,
    Jenny kissed me!

Leigh Hunt.

REMEMBER

REMEMBER it, although you're far away—
    Too far away more fivers yet to land,
    When you no more can proffer notes of
        hand,
Nor I half yearn to change my yea to nay.
Remember, when no more in airy way,
    You tell me of repayment sagely planned:
    Only remember it, you understand!
It's rather late to counsel you to pay;
Yet if you should remember for a while,
    And then forget it wholly, I should grieve;
    For, though your light procrastinations leave
    Small remnants of the hope that once I had,
Than that you should forget your debt and smile,
    I'd rather you'd remember and be sad.

Judy.

[166]

THE WAIL OF THE "PERSONALLY CONDUCTED"

(Chorus heard on the deck of a Saguenay steamboat)

SAPPHICS

INTEGRAL were we, in our old existence;
Separate beings, individually:
Now are our entities blended, fused, and foun-
dered—
We are one person.

We are not mortals, we are not celestials,
We are not birds, the upper ether cleaving,
We are a retrogression toward the monad:
We are Cook's Tourists.

All ways we follow him who holds the guide-book
All things we look at, with bedazzled optics;
Sad are our hearts, because the vulgar rabble
Call us the Cookies.

Happy the man who, by his cheerful fireside,
Says to the partner of his joys and sorrows:
"Anna Maria, let us go to-morrow
Out for an airing."

Him to Manhattan, or the Beach of Brighton,
Gayly he hieth, or if, fate-accursèd,
Lives he in Boston, still he may betake him
Down to Nantasket.

[167]

Happy the mortal free and independent,
Master of the mainspring of his own volition!
Look on us with the eye of sweet compassion:
We are Cook's Tourists.

H. C. Bunner.

CHAIN VERSE

OUT OF SIGHT, OUT OF MIND

THE oft'ner seen, the more I lust,
　　The more I lust, the more I smart,
　　The more I smart, the more I trust,
　　The more I trust, the heavier heart,
The heavy heart breeds mine unrest,
Thy absence therefore I like best.

The rarer seen, the less in mind,
The less in mind, the lesser pain,
The lesser pain, less grief I find,
The lesser grief, the greater gain,
The greater gain, the merrier I,
Therefore I wish thy sight to fly.

The further off, the more I joy,
The more I joy, the happier life,
The happier life, less hurts annoy,
The lesser hurts, pleasure most rife,
Such pleasures rife shall I obtain
When distance doth depart us twain.

Barnaby Googe.

AD MORTEM

THE longer life, the more offence;
 The more offence, the greater pain;
 The greater pain the less defence;
 The less defence, the greater gain—
Wherefore, come death, and let me die!

The shorter life, less care I find,
Less care I take, the sooner over;
The sooner o'er, the merrier mind;
The merrier mind, the better lover—
 Wherefore, come death, and let me die!

Come, gentle death, the ebb of care;
The ebb of care, the flood of life;
The flood of life, I'm sooner there;
I'm sooner there—the end of strife—
The end of strife, that thing wish I—
 Wherefore, come death, and let me die!

       Anonymous.

NERVE THY SOUL

NERVE thy soul with doctrines noble,
 Noble in the walks of time,
 Time that leads to an eternal,
 An eternal life sublime:
Life sublime in moral beauty,
 Beauty that shall ever be;

Ever be to lure thee onward,
  Onward to the fountain free:
Free to every earnest seeker,
  Seeker for the fount of youth,
Youth exultant in its beauty,
  Beauty of the living truth.

                    Anonymous.

CENTONES OR MOSAIC WHIMSEYS

LIFE *

1. Why all this toil for triumphs of an hour?
2. Life's a short summer, man a flower.
3. By turns we catch the vital breath and die—
4. The cradle and the tomb, alas! so nigh.
5. To be, is better far than not to be.
6. Though all man's life may seem a tragedy;
7. But light cares speak when mighty griefs are dumb,
8. The bottom is but shallow whence they come.
9. Your fate is but the common lot of all:
10. Unmingled joys here to no man befall,
11. Nature to each allots his proper sphere;
12. Fortune makes folly her peculiar care;
13. Custom does often reason overrule,
14. And throw a cruel sunshine on a fool.

* 1. Young; 2. Dr. Johnson; 3. Pope; 4. Prior; 5. Sewell; 6. Spenser; 7. Daniell; 8. Sir Walter Raleigh; 9. Longfellow; 10. Southwell; 11. Congreve; 12. Churchill; 13. Rochester; 14. Armstrong; 15. Milton; 16. Bailey; 17. Trench; 18. Somerville; 19. Thomson; 20. Byron; 21. Smollett; 22. Crabbe; 23. Massinger; 24. Cowley; 25. Beattie; 26. Cowper; 27. Sir Walter Davenant; 28. Gray; 29. Willis; 30. Addison; 31. Dryden; 32. Francis Quarles; 33. Watkins; 34. Herrick; 35. William Mason; 36. Hill; 37. Dana; 38. Shakespeare.

15. Live well; how long or short, permit to Heaven;
16. They who forgive us most, shall be most for-
    given.
17. Sin may be clasped so close we cannot see its
    face—
18. Vile intercourse where virtue has no place.
19. Then keep each passion down, however dear;
20. Thou pendulum betwixt a smile and tear.
21. Her sensual snares, let faithless pleasure lay,
22. With craft and skill, to ruin and betray;
23. Soar not too high to fall, but stoop to rise.
24. We masters grow of all that we despise.
25. Oh, then, I renounce that impious self-esteem;
26. Riches have wings, and grandeur is a dream.
27. Think not ambition wise because 'tis brave,
28. The paths of glory lead but to the grave.
29. What is ambition?—'tis a glorious cheat!—
30. Only destructive to the brave and great.
31. What's all the gaudy glitter of a crown?
32. The way to bliss lies not on beds of down.
33. How long we live, not years but actions tell;
34. That man lives twice who lives the first life well.
35. Make, then, while yet we may, your God your
    friend,
36. Whom Christians worship yet not comprehend.
37. The trust that's given guard, and to yourself
    be just;
38. For, live we how we can, yet die we must.

Anonymous.

MY GENEVIEVE *

1. I only knew she came and went,
2.   Like troutlets in a pool;
3. She was a phantom of delight,
4.   And I was like a fool.

5. "One kiss, dear maid," I said, and sighed,
6.   Out of those lips unshorn.
7. She shook her ringlets round her head
8.   And laughed in merry scorn.

9. Ring out, wild bells, to the wild sky,
10.   You heard them, O my heart;
11. 'Tis twelve at night by the castle clock,
12.   Belovèd we must part.

13. "Come back, come back!" she cried in grief,
14.   My eyes are dim with tears—
15. How shall I live through all the days?
16.   All through a hundred years?

17. 'Twas in the prime of summer-time,
18.   She blessed me with her hand;

* 1. Powell; 2. Hood; 3. Wordsworth; 4. Eastman; 5. Coleridge; 6. Longfellow; 7. Stoddard; 8. Tennyson; 9. Tennyson; 10. Alice Cary; 11. Coleridge; 12. Alice Cary; 13. Campbell; 14. Bayard Taylor; 15. Osgood; 16. T. S. Perry; 17. Hood; 18. Hoyt; 19. Edwards; 20. Cornwall; 21. Patmore; 22. Bayard Taylor; 23. Tennyson; 24. Read; 25. Browning; 26. Smith; 27. Coleridge; 28. Wordsworth; 29. Coleridge; 30. Hervey; 31. Wordsworth; 32. Osgood.

19. We strayed together, deeply blest,
20.   Into the dreaming land.

21. The laughing bridal roses blow,
22.   To dress her dark brown hair;
23. My heart is breaking with my woe,
24.   Most beautiful! most rare!

25. I clasped it on her sweet, cold hand,
26.   The precious golden link!
27. I calmed her fears, and she was calm,
28.   "Drink, pretty creature, drink!"

29. And so I won my Genevieve,
30.   And walked in Paradise;
31. The fairest thing that ever grew
32.   Atween me and the skies!

Anonymous.

THE FATE OF THE GLORIOUS DEVIL *

A GLORIOUS devil, large in heart and brain,
    Doomed for a certain term to walk the
        night,
The world forsaking with a calm disdain,
Majestic rises on th' astonished sight.

* 1. Tennyson; 2. Shakespeare; 3. Thomson; 4. Taite; 5. Wordsworth; 6. Pope; 7. Graham; 8. Cowper; 9. Beattie; 10. Rogers; 11. Hemans; 12. Collins; 13. Longfellow; 14. Prior; 15. Beattie; 16. Burns; 17. Wordsworth; 18. Hemans; 19; Crabbe; 20. Chaucer; 21. Collins; 22. Beattie; 23. Gray; 24. Campbell; 25. Bloomfield; 26. Goldsmith; 27. Rogers; 28. Burns; 29. Bloomfield; 30. Byron; 31. Falconer; 32. Thomson; 33. Joanna Baillie; 34. Byron; 35. Shelley; 36. Euripides; 37. Beattie; 38. Hemans; 39. Shakespeare; 40. H. Smith.

Type of the wise who soar, but never roam,—
   Mark how it mounts to man's imperial race!
High is his perch, but humble is his home,
   Fast anchored in the deep abyss of space.

And oft the craggy cliff he loved to climb,
   Where Punch and Scaramouch aloft are seen,
Where Science mounts in radiant car sublime,
   And twilight fairies tread the circled green.

And, borne aloft by the sustaining blast,
   Whom no man fully sees, and none can see,
'Wildered and weary, sits him down at last,
   Beneath the shelter of an aged tree.

I will not stop to tell how far he fled,
   To view the smile of evening on the sea;
He tried to smile, and, half succeeding, said,
   "I smell a loller in the wind," said he.

"What if the lion in his rage I meet?"
   (The Muse interprets thus his tender thought.)
The scourge of Heaven! what terrors round him
     wait!
From planet whirled to planet more remote.

Thence higher still, by countless steps conveyed,
   Remote from towns he ran his godly race;
He lectured every youth that round him played—
   The jostling tears ran down his honest face.

"Another spring!" his heart exulting cries.
  Vain are his weapons, vainer is his force;
A milk-white lion of tremendous size
  Lays him along the snows a stiffened corse.

The haycock rises, and the frequent rake
  Looks on the bleeding foe that made him bleed;
And the green lizard and the golden snake
  Pause at the bold irrevocable deed.

Will ye one transient ray of gladness dart,
  To bid the genial tear of pity flow?
By Heaven! I would rather coin my heart,
  Or Mr. Miller's, commonly called Joe!

                                    Anonymous.

ECHOES *

L ADY Clara Vere de Vere
    Was eight years old she said:
      Every ringlet, lightly shaken, ran
        itself in golden thread.

  She took her little porringer:
  Of me she shall not win renown:
For the baseness of its nature shall have strength
  to drag her down.

  "Sisters and brothers, little Maid?
  There stands the Inspector at thy door:
Like a dog, he hunts for boys who know not two
  and two are four."

* By permission of the Macmillan Company.

"Kind words are more than coronets,"
She said, and wondering looked at me:
"It is the dead unhappy night, and I must hurry
home to tea."

Lewis Carroll.

WHATEVER IS, IS RIGHT

L IVES there a man with soul so dead
Who never to himself has said,
"Shoot folly as it flies"?
Oh! more than tears of blood can tell,
Are in that word, farewell, farewell!
'Tis folly to be wise.

And what is friendship but a name,
That boils on Etna's breast of flame?
Thus runs the world away.
Sweet is the ship that's under sail
To where yon taper cheers the vale,
With hospitable ray!

Drink to me only with thine eyes
Through cloudless climes and starry skies!
My native land, good night!
Adieu, adieu, my native shore;
'Tis Greece, but living Greece no more—
Whatever is, is right!

Laman Blanchard.

JESUITICAL VERSES

THE DOUBLE-FACED CREED

(Read down or across)

I hold for sound faith	What England's church allows,
What Rome's faith saith	My conscience disavows,
Where the king's head	The flock can take no shame
The flock's misled	Who hold the Pope supreme.
Where the altar's dressed	The worship's scarce divine
The people's blessed,	Whose table's bread and wine,
He's but an ass	Who their communion flies
Who shuns the mass	Is catholic and wise.

Anonymous.

EQUIVOCAL VERSES

(Read down or across)

"I love with all my heart	The Tory party here
The Hanoverian part	Most hateful do appear
And for the Settlement	I ever have denied
My conscience gives consent	To be on James's side
Most righteous in the cause	To fight for such a king
To fight for George's laws	Will England's ruin bring
It is my mind and heart	In this opinion I
Though none will take my part	Resolve to live and die."

Anonymous.

[179]

THE PLATFORM

(Read down or across)

Hurrah for	The old Union
Secession	Is a curse
We fight for	The Constitution
The Confederacy	Is a league with hell
We love	Free speech
The rebellion	Is treason
We glory in	A free press
Separation	Will not be tolerated
We fight not for	The negro's freedom
Reconstruction	Must be obtained
We must succeed	At every hazard
The Union	We love
We love not	The negro
We never said	Let the Union slide
We want	The Union as it was
Foreign intervention	Is played out
We cherish	The old flag
The stars and bars	Is a flaunting lie
We venerate	The habeas corpus
Southern chivalry	Is hateful
Death to	Jeff Davis
Abe Lincoln	Isn't the Government
Down with	Mob law
Law and order	Shall triumph.

Anonymous.

PANEGYRIC ON THE LADIES

(Read alternate lines)

THAT man must lead a happy life
    Who's free from matrimonial chains,
Who is directed by a wife
    Is sure to suffer for his pains.

Adam could find no solid peace
    When Eve was given for a mate;
Until he saw a woman's face
    Adam was in a happy state.

In all the female race appear
    Hypocrisy, deceit, and pride;
Truth, darling of a heart sincere,
    In woman never did reside.

What tongue is able to unfold
    The failings that in woman dwell?
The worth in woman we behold
    Is almost imperceptible.

Confusion take the man, I say,
    Who changes from his singleness,
Who will not yield to woman's sway
    Is sure of earthly blessedness.

Anonymous.

[181]

AMBIGUOUS LINES

(Read with a comma after the first noun in each line)

I saw a peacock with a fiery tail
I saw a blazing comet pour down hail
I saw a cloud all wrapt with ivy round
I saw a lofty oak creep on the ground
I saw a beetle swallow up a whale
I saw a foaming sea brimful of ale
I saw a pewter cup sixteen feet deep
I saw a well full of men's tears that weep
I saw wet eyes in flames of living fire
I saw a house as high as the moon and higher
I saw the glorious sun at deep midnight
I saw the man who saw this wondrous sight.

I saw a pack of cards gnawing a bone
I saw a dog seated on Britain's throne
I saw King George shut up within a box
I saw an orange driving a fat ox
I saw a butcher not a twelvemonth old
I saw a great-coat all of solid gold
I saw two buttons telling of their dreams
I saw my friends who wished I'd quit these themes.

Anonymous.

ECHO VERSES

ECHO

I ASKED of Echo, t'other day
    (Whose words are often few and funny),
  What to a novice she could say
    Of courtship, love, and matrimony.
    Quoth Echo plainly,—"Matter-o'-money!"

Whom should I marry? Should it be
  A dashing damsel, gay and pert,
A pattern of inconstancy;
  Or selfish, mercenary flirt?
  Quoth Echo, sharply,—"Nary flirt!"

What if, aweary of the strife
  That long has lured the dear deceiver,
She promise to amend her life,
  And sin no more; can I believe her?
  Quoth Echo, very promptly,—"Leave her!"

But if some maiden with a heart
  On me should venture to bestow it,
Pray, should I act the wiser part
  To take the treasure or forego it?
  Quoth Echo, with decision,—"Go it!"

But what if, seemingly afraid
  To bind her fate in Hymen's fetter,
She vow she means to die a maid,
  In answer to my loving letter?
  Quoth Echo, rather coolly,—"Let her!"

What if, in spite of her disdain,
  I find my heart intwined about
With Cupid's dear delicious chain
  So closely that I can't get out?
  Quoth Echo, laughingly,—"Get out!"

But if some maid with beauty blest,
  As pure and fair as Heaven can make her,
Will share my labor and my rest
  Till envious Death shall overtake her?
  Quoth Echo (sotto voce),—"Take her!"

                              John G. Saxe.

ROYALIST LINES

WHAT wantest thou, that thou art in this
    sad taking?
                        Echo: A king.
What made him first remove hence his residing?
                        Siding.
Did any here deny him satisfaction?
                        Faction.
Tell me wherein the strength of faction lies?
                        On lies.
What didst thou when the king left his Parlia-
    ment?
                        Lament.

What terms wouldst give to gain his company?
            Any.
What wouldst thou do if here thou mightst be-
    hold him?
                    Hold him.
But wouldst thou save him with thy best endeav-
    our?
                    Ever.
But if he comes not, what becomes of London?
                Undone.
                        Anonymous.

SONG

ECHO, tell me, while I wander
        O'er this fairy plain to prove him,
    If my shepherd still grows fonder,
        Ought I in return to love him?
    Echo: Love him, love him!

If he loves, as is the fashion,
    Should I churlishly forsake him?
Or in pity to his passion,
    Fondly to my bosom take him?
    Echo: Take him, take him!

Thy advice then, I'll adhere to,
    Since in Cupid's chains I've led him;
And with Henry shall not fear to
    Marry, if you answer, "Wed him!"
    Echo: Wed him, wed him!
                        Addison.

[185]

MACARONIC POETRY

VERY FELIS-ITOUS

FELIS sedit by a hole,
   Intente she, cum omni soul,
            Predere rats.
   Mice cucurrerunt trans the floor,
In numero duo tres or more,
            Obliti cats.

Felis saw them oculis,
"I'll have them," inquit she, "I guess,
            Dum ludunt."
Tunc illa crepit toward the group,
"Habeam" dixit, "good rat soup—
            Pingues sunt."

Mice continued all ludere,
Intenti they in ludum vere,
            Gaudenter.
Tunc rushed the felis into them,
Et tore them omnes limb from limb,
            Violenter.

MORAL

Mures omnes, nunc be shy,
Et aurem præbe mihi—
            Benigne:
Sic hoc satis—"verbum sat,"
Avoid a whopping Thomas cat
            Studiose.
                    Green Kendrick.

ÆSTIVATION

IN candent ire the solar splendour flames;
  The foles, languescent, pend from arid rames;
  His humid front the cive, anheling, wipes,
  And dreams of erring on ventiferous ripes.

How dulce to vive occult to mortal eyes,
Dorm on the herb with none to supervise,
Carp the suave berries from the crescent vine,
And bibe the flow from longicaudate kine!

To me, alas! no verdurous visions come,
Save yon exiguous pool's conferva-scum—
No concave vast repeats the tender hue
That laves my milk-jug with celestial blue.

Me wretched! let me curr to quercine shades!
Effund your albid hausts, lactiferous maids!
Oh, might I vole to some umbrageous clump,—
Depart—be off,—excede,—evade,—crump!
                    Oliver Wendell Holmes.

[187]

CE MÊME VIEUX COON

CE même vieux coon n'est pas quite mort,
　Il n'est pas seulement napping:
Je pense, myself, unless j'ai tort,
　Cette chose est yet to happen.

En dix-huit forty-four, je sais,
　Vous'll hear des curious noises;
He'll whet ses dents against some Clay,
　Et scare des Loco—Bois-es!

You know qui quand il est awake,
　Et quand il scratch ses clawses,
Les Locos dans leurs souliers shake,
　Et, sheepish, hang leurs jaws-es.

Ce même vieux coon je ne sais pas why,
　Le mischief's come across him,
Il fait believe he's going to die,
　Quand seulement playing 'possum.

Mais wait till nous le want encore,
　Nous'll stir him with une pole;
He'll bite as mauvais as before
　Nous pulled him de son hole!

Anonymous.

WILD SPORTS IN THE EAST

ARMA virumque cano qui primo solebo peep-
    ing,
        Jam nunc cum tabbynox languet to but-
        ton her eyelids,
Cum pointers et spaniels campos sylvasque per-
    errant.
Vos mihi—Brontothesi over arms small and great
    dominantes,
Date spurs to dull poet qui dog Latin carmina
    condit,
Artibus atque novis audax dum sportsman I follow
Per stubbles et turnips et tot discrimina rerum,
Dum partridge with popping terrificare minantur
Pauci, namque valent a feather tangere plumbo!
Carmina si hang fire discharge them bag-piping
    Apollo.
Te quoque, magne cleator, te memorande pre-
    camur.
Jam nunc thy fame gallops super Garamantos et
    Indos,
Nam nabobs nil nisi de brimstone et charcoal
    loquentur,
Horriferifizque "Tippoo" sulphurea, sustinet arma.
Induit ecce shooter tunicam made of neat marble
    drugget,
Quæ bene convenient defluxit to the waistband
    of breeches,
Nunc paper et powder et silices popped in the
    side-pocket,

Immemor haud shot-bag graditur comitatus two
    pointers,
Mellorian retinens tormentum dextra bibarelled:
En stat staunch dog Dingo haud aliter quam
    steady guide post,
Proximus atque Pero per stat si ponere juxta,
With gun cocked and levelled at æva lumine clauso,
Nunc avicida resolves haud double strong par-
    cere powder.
Van teneri yelpers vos grandivique parentes
Nunc palsy pate Jove orate to dress to the left
    hand,
Et Veneri tip the wink like a shot to skim down
    ab alto
Mingere per touch-hole totamque madescere prim-
    ing.
Nunc lugete dire nunc sportsman plangite palmas,
Ex silis ecce lepus from box cum thistle aperto!
Bang bellowed both barrels, heu! pronus sterni-
    tur each dog,
Et puss in the interim creeps away sub tegmine
    thornbush.

Anonymous.

TO THE FAIR "COME-OUTER"

LADY! formosissima tu!
    Cæruleis oculis have you,
      Ditto nose!
Et vous n'avez pas une faute—
And that you are going to vote,
    Goodness knows!

[190]

And the roseus on your cheek,
And your Algebra and Greek,
      Are parfait!
And your jactus oculi
Knows each star that shines in the
      Milky Way!

You have pouting, piquant lips,
Sans doute vous pouvez an eclipse
      Calculate!
Ne Cærulum colorantur,
I should have in you, instanter,
      Met my fate!

Si, by some arrangement dual,
I at once were Kant and Whewell;
      It would pay—
Procus noti then to come
To so sweet an Artium
      Magistra!

Or, Jewel of Consistency,
Si possem clear-starch, cookere,
      Votre learning
Might the leges proscribere—
Do the pro patria mori,
      I, the churning!
               Anonymous

"ICH BIN DEIN"

IN tempus old a hero lived,
    Qui loved puellas deux;
He ne pouvait pas quite to say
    Which one amabat mieux.

Dit-il lui-même, un beau matin,
    Non 'possum both avoir,
Sed si address Amanda Ann,
    Then Kate and I have war.

Amanda habet argent coin,
    Sed Kate has aureas curls;
Et both sunt very ἀγαθά,
    Et quite formosa girls.

Enfin, the youthful anthropos,
    Φιλοῦν the duo maids,
Resolved proponere ad Kate
    Devant cet evening's shades.

Procedens then to Kate's domo,
    Il trouve Amanda there;
Καὶ quite forgot his good resolves
    Both sunt so goodly fair.

Sed, smiling on the new tapis,
    Between the puellas twain,
Cœpit to tell his flame to Kate
    Dans un poetique strain.

[192]

Mais, glancing ever and anon
  At fair Amanda's eyes,
Illæ non possunt dicere,
  Pro which he meant his sighs.

Each virgo heard the demi vow
  With cheeks as rouge as wine,
And offering each a milk-white hand,
  Both whispered, "Ich bin dein!"
                              Anonymous.

MACARONIC MOTHER GOOSE

JACK AND JILL

JACK cum amico Jill,
    Ascendit super montem;
  Johannes cecedit down the hill,
    Ex forte fregit frontem.

LITTLE BO-PEEP

  Parvula Bo-peep
  Amisit her sheep,
Et nescit where to find 'em;
  Desere alone,
  Et venient home,
Cum omnibus caudis behind 'em.

[193]

LITTLE JACK HORNER

Parvus Jacobus Horner
Sedebat in corner,
Edens a Christmas pie;
Inferuit thumb,
Extraherit plum—
Clamans, "Quid sharp puer am I!"

Anonymous.

LINGUISTIC AND DIALECTIC VERSE

YE CARPETTE KNYGHTE *

I HAVE a horse—a ryghte good horse—
   Ne doe I envie those
Who scoure ye plaine in headie course,
   Tyll soddaine on theyre nose
They lyghte wyth unexpected force—
   It ys—a horse of clothes.

I have a saddel—"Say'st thou soe?
   With styrruppes, Knyghte, to boote?"
I sayde not that—I answere "Noe"—
   Yt lacketh such, I woot—
It ys a mutton-saddel, loe!
   Parte of ye fleecie brute.

I have a bytte—ayghte good bytte—
   As schall bee seene in tyme.
Ye jawe of horse yt wyll not fytte—
   Yts use ys more sublyme.
Fayre Syr, how deemest thou of yt?
   Yt ys—thys bytte of rhyme.

Lewis Carroll.

* By permission of the Macmillan Company.

THE CARELESSE NURSE MAYD

I SAWE a Mayd sitte on a Bank,
  Beguiled by wooer fayne and fond!
  And whiles His flatterynge Vowes She drank
  Her Nurselynge slipt within a Pond!

All Even Tide they Talkde and Kist,
For She was Fayre and He was Kinde;
The Sunne went down before She wist
Another Sonne had sett behinde!

With angrie Hands and frownynge Browe,
That deemed Her own the Urchine's Sinne,
She pluckt Him out, but he was nowe
Past being Whipt for fallynge in.

She then beginnes to wayle the Ladde
With Shrikes that Echo answered round—
O foolishe Mayd! to be soe sadde
The Momente that her care was drownd!

Thomas Hood.

A BORDER BALLAD *

J AMIE lad, I lo'e ye weel,
  Jamie lad, I lo'e nae ither,
  Jamie lad, I lo'e ye weel,
    Like a mither.

* From "More Misrepresentative Men," copyrighted, 1905, by
Fox, Duffield & Co.

[196]

Jamie's ganging doon the burn,
Jamie's ganging doon, whateffer,
Jamie's ganging doon the burn,
    To Strathpeffer!

Jamie's comin' hame to dee,
Jamie's comin' hame, I'm thinkin',
Jamie's comin' hame to dee,
    Dee o' drinkin'!

Hech! Jamie! Losh! Jamie!
 Dinna greet sae sair!
Gin ye canna, winna, shanna
 See yer lassie mair!
    Wha' hoo!
    Wha' hae!
    Strathpeffer!

The queys are moopin' i' the mirk,
An' gin ye thole abin' the kirk,
I'll gar ye tocher hame fra' work,
    Sae straught an' prinsie;
In vain the lavrock leaves the snaw,
The sonsie cowslips blithely blaw,
The elbucks wheep adoon the shaw,
    Or warl a whimsy,

The cootie muircocks crousely craw,
The maukins tak' their fud fu' braw,
I gie their wanes a random paw,
    For a' they're skilpy;

[197]

For wha' sae glaikit, gleg an' din,
To but the ben, or loup the linn,
Or scraw aboon the tirlin'-pin
    Sae frae an' gilpie?

Och, snood the sporran roun' ma lap,
The cairngorm clap in ilka cap,
    Och, hand me o'er
    Ma lang claymore,
    Twa bannocks an' a bap,
      Wha hoo!
    Twa bannocks an' a bap!
        Captain Harry Graham.

VILLIKENS *

QUAND VILLIKINS se promenait dans son
    jardin un matin,
    Il decouvrit La Belle Dinah étendue sur
    son chemin,
Une tasse de soupe poisonnée froide dans sa main
Et un billet-doux lisant qu'elle s'était suicidée
    bien.

Le corpus rigide il l'embrassait mille fois;
D'être separé de sa Dinah il ne l'endurait pas;
Il avalait le reste de la soupe exécrable
Et fut enterré de suite avec sa Dinah aimable.

* From " Blown Away," by Richard Mansfield, copyrighted, 1897,
by L. C. Page & Co. (Inc.).

[198]

Entendez bien la morale de ma plainte:
D'un amant vulgaire il se change donc en saint,
Et pour toute demoiselle qui se tue par amour,
Qu'il meurt en martyr un jeune bel-homme
    toujours!

             Richard Mansfield.

FROM VIVETTE'S "MILKMAID"

A MAYDE ther was, semely and meke enow
    She sate a-milken of a purpil Cowe;
    Rosy hire cheke as in the Month of Maye
    And sikerly her merry Songe was gay
As of the Larke vprist, washen in Dewe;
Like Shene of Sterres sperkled hire Eyen two.
Now came ther by that Way, a hendy Knight
The Mayde espien in morwening Light.
A faire Perfon he was—of Corage trewe
With lusty Berd and Chekes of rody Hewe;
Dere Ladye (quod he) far and wide I've straied
Uncouthe Aventure in strange Contree made
Fro Berwike vnto Ware. Parde I vowe
Erewhiles I never sawe a purpil Cowe!
Fayn wold I knowe how Catel thus can be?
Tel me I praie you, of yore Courtesie!
The Mayde hire Milken stent.—Goode Sir she faide
The Master's Mandement on vs ylaid
Decrees that in these yclept gilden Houres
Hys Kyne shall ete of nought but Vylet Floures!

             Carolyn Wells.

TRIOLETS OLLENDORFFIENS

JE suis le frère
   Du bon cocher;
   Où est sa mère?
   Je suis le frère.
Tu es le père
Je suis le frère
Du jardinier
Du bon cocher.

Où est mon canif?
J'ai perdu ma chatte.
Je veux du rosbif.
Où est mon canif?
J'ai tué le Juif.
Faut-il qu'on se batte?
Où est mon canif?
J'ai perdu ma chatte.

La belle cousine
Du fils de ma bru
Vit dans ma cuisine,
La belle cousine!
Ta laide voisine
N'a jamais connu
La belle cousine
Du fils de ma bru.

J. K. Stephen.

JUSTICE TO SCOTLAND

(An unpublished poem by Burns)

O MICKLE yeuks the keckle doup,
    An' a' unsicker girns the graith,
For wae and wae! the crowdies loup
    O'er jouk an' hallan, braw an' baith
Where ance the coggie hirpled fair,
  And blithesome poortith toomed the loof,
There's nae a burnie giglet rare
  But blaws in ilka jinking coof.

The routhie bield that gars the gear
  Is gone where glint the pawky een.
And aye the stound is birkin lear
  Where sconnered yowies wheeped yestreen,
The creeshie rax wi' skelpin' kaes
  Nae mair the howdie bicker whangs,
Nor weanies in their wee bit claes
  Glour light as lammies wi' their sangs.

Yet leeze me on my bonny byke!
  My drappie aiblins blinks the noo,
An' leesome luve has lapt the dyke
  Forgatherin' just a wee bit fou.
And Scotia! while thy rantin' lunt
  Is mirk and moop with gowans fine,
I'll stowlins pit my unco brunt,
  An' cleek my duds for auld lang syne.

                         Punch.

"SOLDIER, REST!"

A RUSSIAN sailed over the blue Black Sea
    Just when the war was growing hot,
And he shouted, "I'm Tjalikavakeree—
Karindabrolikanavandorot—
      Schipkadirova—
      Ivandiszstova—
        Sanilik—
        Danilik—
      Varagobhot!"

A Turk was standing upon the shore
    Right where the terrible Russian crossed;
And he cried, "Bismillah! I'm Abd el Kor—
Bazaroukilgonautoskobrosk—
      Getzinpravadi—
        Grivido—
        Blivido—
      Jenikodosk!"

So they stood like brave men, long and well,
    And they called each other their proper names,
Till the lockjaw seized them, and where they fell
    They buried them both by the Irdosholames—
      Kalatalustchuk—
      Mischaribustchup—
        Bulgari—
        Dulgari—
      Sagharimainz.

Robert J. Burdette.

[202]

PUNNING WHIMSEYS

THE BEAUTIES OF ENGLISH ORTHOGRAPHY

A PRETTY deer is dear to me,
    A hare with downy hair,
A hart I love with all my heart,
    But barely bear a bear.

'Tis plain that no one takes a plane,
    To have a pair of pears,
Although a rake may take a rake,
    To tear away the tares.

A scribe in writing right may write,
    May write and still be wrong;
For write and rite are neither right,
    And don't to right belong.

Robertson is not Robert's son,
    Nor did he rob Burt's son,
Yet Robert's sun is Robin's sun,
    And everybody's sun.

Beer often brings a bier to man,
  Coughing a coffin brings,
And too much ale will make us ail,
  As well as other things.

The person lies who says he lies,
  When he is not reclining;
And when consumptive folk decline,
  They all decline declining.

Quails do not quail before the storm,
  A bow will bow before it;
We cannot rein the rain at all—
  No earthly power reigns o'er it.

The dyer dyes a while, then dies—
  To dye he's always trying;
Until upon his dying bed
  He thinks no more of dyeing.

A son of Mars mars many a son,
  And Deys must have their days;
And every knight should pray each night
  To Him who weighs his ways.

'Tis meet that man should mete out meat
  To feed one's future son;
The fair should fare on love alone,
  Else one cannot be won.

The springs shoot forth each spring, and shoots
   Shoot forward one and all;
Though summer kills the flowers, it leaves
   The leaves to fall in fall.

I would a story here commence,
   But you might think it stale;
So we'll suppose that we have reached
   The tail end of our tale.

                  Anonymous.

THE BRIEFLESS BARRISTER

(*A Ballad*)

AN Attorney was taking a turn,
   In shabby habiliments drest;
   His coat it was shockingly worn,
     And the rust had invested his vest.

His breeches had suffered a breach,
   His linen and worsted were worse;
He had scarce a whole crown in his hat.
   And not half-a-crown in his purse.

And thus as he wandered along,
   A cheerless and comfortless elf,
He sought for relief in a song,
   Or complainingly talked to himself:

"Unfortunate man that I am!
    I've never a client but grief;
The case is, I've no case at all,
    And in brief, I've ne'er had a brief!

"I've waited and waited in vain,
    Expecting an 'opening' to find,
Where an honest young lawyer might gain
    Some reward for the toil of his mind.

"'Tis not that I'm wanting in law,
    Or lack an intelligent face,
That others have cases to plead,
    While I have to plead for a case.

"Oh, how can a modest young man,
    E'er hope for the smallest progression—
The profession's already so full
    Of lawyers so full of profession!"

While thus he was strolling around,
    His eye accidentally fell
On a very deep hole in the ground,
    And he sighed to himself, "It is well!"

To curb his emotions, he sat
    On the curb-stone the space of a minute,
Then cried, "Here's an opening at last!"
    And in less than a jiffy was in it!

Next morning twelve citizens came
    ('Twas the coroner bade them attend),
To the end that it might be determined
    How the man had determined his end!

"The man was a lawyer, I hear,"
  Quoth the foreman who sat on the corse;
"A lawyer? Alas!" said another,
  "Undoubtedly died of remorse!"

A third said, "He knew the deceased,
  An attorney well versed in the laws,
And as to the cause of his death,
  'Twas no doubt from the want of a cause."

The jury decided at length,
  After solemnly weighing the matter,
"That the lawyer was drownded, because
  He could not keep his head above water!"
                                    John G. Saxe.

A COUNTRY SUMMER PASTORAL

(*As written by a learned scholar of the city from knowledge derived from etymological deductions rather than from actual experience*)

I WOULD flee from the city's rule and law,
    From its fashion and form cut loose,
  And go where the strawberry grows on its
      straw,
    And the gooseberry on its goose;
Where the catnip tree is climbed by the cat
  As she crouches for her prey—
The guileless and unsuspecting rat
  On the rattan bush at play.

I will watch at ease for the saffron cow
  And the cowlet in their glee,
As they leap in joy from bough to bough
  On the top of the cowslip tree;
Where the musical partridge drums on his drum,
  And the woodchuck chucks his wood,
And the dog devours the dog-wood plum
  In the primitive solitude.

And then to the whitewashed dairy I'll turn,
  Where the dairymaid hastening hies,
Her ruddy and golden-haired butter to churn
  From the milk of her butterflies;
And I'll rise at morn with the early bird,
  To the fragrant farm-yard pass,
When the farmer turns his beautiful herd
  Of grasshoppers out to grass.

Anonymous.

JAPANESQUE *

OH, where the white quince blossom swings
    I love to take my Japan ease!
    I love the maid Anise who clings
      So lightly on my Japan knees;
I love the little song she sings,
  The little love-song Japanese.
I *almost* love the lute's *tink-tunkle*
  Played by that charming Jap Anise—
For am I not her old Jap uncle?
  And is she not my Japan niece?

Oliver Herford.

* From " The Bashful Earthquake," published by Charles Scribner's
Sons.

TO MY NOSE

KNOWS he that never took a pinch,
    Nosey, the pleasure thence which flows,
    Knows he the titillating joys
        Which my nose knows?
O Nose, I am as proud of thee
As any mountain of its snows,
I gaze on thee, and feel that pride
        A Roman knows!

Alfred A. Forrester (Alfred Crowquil).

A CATALECTIC MONODY!

A CAT I sing, of famous memory,
    Though catachrestical my song may be;
    In a small garden catacomb she lies,
And cataclysms fill her comrades' eyes;
Borne on the air, the catacoustic song,
Swells with her virtues' catalogue along;
No cataplasm could lengthen out her years,
Though mourning friends shed cataracts of tears.
Once loud and strong her catechist-like voice
It dwindled to a catcall's squeaking noise;
Most categorical her virtues shone,
By catenation join'd each one to one;—
But a vile catchpoll dog, with cruel bite,
Like catling's cut, her strength disabled quite;

[209]

Her caterwauling pierced the heavy air,
As cataphracts their arms through legions bear;
'Tis vain! as caterpillars drag away
Their lengths, like cattle after busy day,
She ling'ring died, nor left in kit-kat the
Embodyment of this catastrophe.

Cruikshank's Omnibus.

SPELLING REFORM

WITH tragic air the love-lorn heir
    Once chased the chaste Louise;
  She quickly guessed her guest was there
    To please her with his pleas.

Now at her side he kneeling sighed,
    His sighs of woeful size;
"Oh, hear me here, for lo, most low
    I rise before your eyes.

"This soul is sole thine own, Louise—
    'Twill never wean, I ween,
The love that I for aye shall feel,
    Though mean may be its mien!"

"You know I cannot tell you no,"
    The maid made answer true;
"I love you aught, as sure I ought—
    To you 'tis due I do!"

"Since you are won, oh fairest one,
  The marriage rite is right—
The chapel aisle I'll lead you up
  This night," exclaimed the knight.

Anonymous.

TRAVESTIES

OPTIMISM

BE brave, faint heart,
    The dough shall yet be cake;
Be strong, weak heart,
    The butter is to come.
Some cheerful chance will right the apple-cart,
The devious pig will gain the lucky mart,
    Loquacity be dumb,—
    Collapsed the fake.
Be brave, faint heart!

Be strong, weak heart,
    The path will be made plain;
Be brave, faint heart,
    The bore will crawl away.
The upside down will turn to right side up,
The stiffened lip compel that slipping cup,
    The doldrums of the day
    Be not in vain.
Be strong, weak heart!

Be brave, faint heart,
    The jelly means to jell;
Be strong, weak heart,
    The hopes are in the malt.

The wrong side in will yet turn right side out,
The long-time lost come down yon cormorant spout.
      Life still is worth her salt:
      What ends well's well.
    Be brave, faint heart!

N. M.

THE ORIGINAL LAMB

OH, Mary had a little lamb, regarding whose
    cuticular
    The fluff exterior was white and kinked in
    each particular.
On each occasion when the lass was seen per-
    ambulating,
The little quadruped likewise was there a gallivating.

One day it did accompany her to the knowledge
    dispensary,
Which to every rule and precedent was recklessly
    contrary.
Immediately whereupon the pedagogue superior,
Exasperated, did eject the lamb from the interior.

Then Mary, on beholding such performance
    arbitrary,
Suffused her eyes with saline drops from glands
    called lachrymary,
And all the pupils grew thereat tumultuously hilari-
    ous,
And speculated on the case with wild conjectures
    various.

[213]

"What makes the lamb love Mary so?" the scholars
   asked the teacher.
He paused a moment, then he tried to diagnose the
   creature.
"Oh pecus amorem Mary habit omnia temporum."
"Thanks, teacher dear," the scholars cried, and
   awe crept darkly o'er 'em.

Tid-bits.

THE LITTLE STAR

SCINTILLATE scintillate, globule orific,
   Fain would I fathom thy nature's specific.
   Loftily poised in ether capacious,
   Strongly resembling a gem carbonaceous.

When torrid Phœbus refuses his presence
And ceases to lamp with fierce incandescence,
Then you illumine the regions supernal,
Scintillate, scintillate, semper nocturnal.

Then the victim of hospiceless peregrination
Gratefully hails your minute coruscation.
He could not determine his journey's direction
But for your bright scintillating protection.

Anonymous.

A PIAZZA TRAGEDY

THE beauteous Ethel's father has a
    Newly painted front piazza—
      He has a
      Piazza;
When with tobacco juice 'twas tainted
They had the front piazza painted—
      That tainted
      Piazza painted.

Algernon called that night, perchance,
Arrayed in comely sealskin pants—
      That night, perchance,
      In gorgeous pants;
Engaging Ethel in a chat
On that piazza down he sat—
      In chat,
      They sat.

And when an hour or two had pass'd,
He tried to rise, but oh! stuck fast—
      At last
      Stuck fast!
Fair Ethel shrieked, "It is the paint!"
And fainted in a deadly faint—
      This saint
      Did faint.

[215]

Algernon sits there till this day—
He cannot tear himself away,—
    Away?
    Nay, nay!
His pants are firm, the paint is dry—
He's nothing else to do but die—
    To die!
    O my!

Eugene Field.

AFTER DILETTANTE CONCETTI

"WHY do you wear your hair like a man,
    Sister Helen?
    This week is the third since you began."
"I'm writing a ballad; be still if you can,
    Little brother.
    (O Mother Carey, mother!
What chickens are these between sea and heaven?)"

"But why does your figure appear so lean,
    Sister Helen?
And why do you dress in sage, sage green?"
"Children should never be heard, if seen,
    Little brother?
    (O Mother Carey, mother!
What fowls are a-wing in the stormy heaven!)"

"But why is your face so yellowy white,
    Sister Helen?

And why are your skirts so funnily tight?"
"Be quiet, you torment, or how can I write,
        Little brother?
        (O Mother Carey, mother!
How gathers thy train to the sea from the heaven!)'

"And who's Mother Carey, and what is her train,
        Sister Helen?
And why do you call her again and again?"
"You troublesome boy, why that's the refrain,
        Little brother.
        (O Mother Carey, mother!
What work is toward in the startled heaven?)"

"And what's a refrain?   What a curious word,
        Sister Helen!
Is the ballad you're writing about a sea-bird?"
"Not at all; why should it be?   Don't be absurd,
        Little brother.
        (O Mother Carey, mother!
Thy brood flies lower as lowers the heaven.)"

        (A big brother speaketh:)
"The refrain you've studied a meaning had,
        Sister Helen!
It gave strange force to a weird ballad.
But refrains have become a ridiculous 'fad,'
        Little brother.
        And Mother Carey, mother,
Has a bearing on nothing in earth or heaven.

[217]

"But the finical fashion has had its day,
        Sister Helen.
And let's try in the style of a different lay
To bid it adieu in poetical way,
        Little brother.
      So, Mother Carey, mother!
Collect your chickens and go to—heaven."

*(A pause. Then the big brother singeth, accompany-
ing himself in a plaintive wise on the triangle.)*

"Look in my face.   My name is Used-to-was;
    I am also called Played-out, and Done to Death,
    And It-will-wash-no-more.   Awakeneth
Slowly but sure awakening it has,
The common-sense of man; and I, alas!
    The ballad-burden trick, now known too well,
    Am turned to scorn, and grown contemptible—
A too transparent artifice to pass.

"What a cheap dodge I am!   The cats who dart
    Tin-kettled through the streets in wild surprise
    Assail judicious ears not otherwise;
And yet no critics praise the urchin's 'art,'
Who to the wretched creature's caudal part
    Its foolish empty-jingling 'burden' ties."
                 H. D. Traill.

ISRAFIDDLESTRINGS

IN heaven a Spirit doth dwell
  Whose heart strings are a fiddle,
 (The reason he sings so well—
This fiddler Israfel),
And the giddy stars (will any one tell
Why giddy?) to attend his spell
 Cease their hymns in the middle.

On the height of her go
 Totters the Moon, and blushes
 As the song of that fiddle rushes
Across her bow.
The red Lightning stands to listen,
And the eyes of the Pleiads glisten
As each of the seven puts its fist in
Its eyes, for the mist in.

And they say—it's a riddle—
 That all these listening things,
That stop in the middle
For the heart-strung fiddle
 With such the Spirit sings,
Are held as on the griddle
 By these unusual strings.

Wherefore thou art not wrong,
 Israfel! in that thou boastest
Fiddlestrings uncommon strong;
To thee the fiddlestrings belong
 With which thou toastest
Other hearts as on a prong.

[219]

Yes! heaven is thine, but this
  Is a world of sours and sweets,—
   Where cold meats are cold meats,
And the eater's most perfect bliss
  Is the shadow of him who treats.

If I could griddle
As Israfiddle
  Has griddled—he fiddle as I,—
He might not fiddle so wild a riddle
  As this mad melody,
While the Pleiads all would leave off in the middle
  Hearing my griddle-cry.

                       Anonymous.

MIDSUMMER MADNESS

(A Soliloquy)

I AM a hearthrug—
   Yes, a rug—
     Though I cannot describe myself as snug;
Yet I know that for me they paid a price
For a Turkey carpet that would suffice
(But we live in an age of rascal vice).
   Why was I ever woven,
For a clumsy lout, with a wooden leg,
To come with his endless Peg! Peg!
    Peg! Peg!
   With a wooden leg,
Till countless holes I'm drove in.

("Drove," I have said, and it should be "driven";
A heartrug's blunders should be forgiven,
For wretched scribblers have exercised
     Such endless bosh and clamour,
So improvidently have improvised,
That they've utterly ungrammaticised
     Our ungrammatical grammar).
          And the coals
          Burn holes,
          Or make spots like moles,
And my lily-white tints, as black as your hat turn,
And the housemaid (a matricide, will-forging
     slattern),
     Rolls
     The rolls
     From the plate, in shoals,
When they're put to warm in front of the coals;
And no one with me condoles,
For the butter stains on my beautiful pattern.
But the coals and rolls, and sometimes soles,
Dropp'd from the frying-pan out of the fire,
Are nothing to raise my indignant ire,
     Like the Peg! Peg!
Of that horrible man with the wooden leg.

     This moral spread from me,
        Sing it, ring it, yelp it—
     Never a hearthrug be,
        That is if you can help it.

                                   Anonymous.

BALLAD OF THE CANAL

WE were crowded in the cabin,
  Not a soul had room to sleep;
It was midnight on the waters,
  And the banks were very steep.

'Tis a fearful thing when sleeping
  To be startled by the shock,
And to hear the rattling trumpet
  Thunder, "Coming to a lock!"

So we shuddered there in silence,
  For the stoutest berth was shook,
While the wooden gates were opened
  And the mate talked with the cook.

And as thus we lay in darkness,
  Each one wishing we were there,
"We are through!" the captain shouted,
  And he sat down on a chair.

And his little daughter whispered,
  Thinking that he ought to know,
"Isn't travelling by canal-boats
  Just as safe as it is slow?"

Then he kissed the little maiden,
  And with better cheer we spoke,
And we trotted into Pittsburg,
  When the morn looked through the smoke.
                              Phoebe Cary.

POETRY AND THE POET *
(*A Sonnet*)

(Found on the Poet's desk)

WEARY, I open wide the antique pane
      I ope to the air
    I ope to
I open to the air the antique pane
   And gaze { beyond? / across } the thrift-sown fields of
     wheat, (commonplace?)
  A-shimmering green in breezes born of heat;
And lo!
And high

And my soul's eyes behold { a?- / the } billowy main

Whose further shore is Greece   strain
                                 again
                                 vain
(Arcadia—mythological allusion. — Mem.: Lemprière.)
  I see thee, Atalanta, vestal fleet,
And look! with doves low-fluttering round her feet,

Comes Venus through the golden { fields of? / bowing } grain

---

* From Poems of H. C. Bunner, by permission of Charles Scribner's Sons.

(Heard by the Poet's neighbor)
Venus be bothered—it's Virginia Dix!

(Found on the Poet's door)
Out on important business—back at 6.
                                        H. C. Bunner.

WHENCENESS OF THE WHICH
(Some distance after Tennyson)

COME into the Whenceness Which,
      For the fierce Because has flown:
Come into the Whenceness Which,
      I am here by the Where alone;
And the Whereas odors are wafted abroad
   Till I hold my nose and groan.

Queen Which of the Whichbud garden of What's
   Come hither the jig is done.
In gloss of Isness and shimmer of Was,
   Queen Thisness and Which is one;
Shine out, little Which, sunning over the bangs,
   To the Nowness, and be its sun.

There has fallen a splendid tear
   From the Is flower at the fence;
She is coming, my Which, my dear,
   And as she Whistles a song of the Whence,
The Nowness cries, "She is near, she is near."
   And the Thingness howls, "Alas!"
The Whoness murmurs, "Well, I should smile,"
   And the Whatlet sobs, "I pass."
                                        Anonymous.

[224]

THE MIGHTY MUST

COME mighty Must!
  Inevitable Shall!
 In thee I trust.
   Time weaves my coronal!
Go mocking Is!
 Go disappointing Was!
That I am this
 Ye are the cursed cause!
Yet humble second shall be first,
   I ween;
And dead and buried be the curst
   Has Been!

Oh weak Might Be!
 Oh, May, Might, Could, Would, Should!
How powerless ye
 For evil or for good!
In every sense
 Your moods I cheerless call,
Whate'er your tense
 Ye are imperfect, all!
Ye have deceived the trust I've shown
   In ye!
Away! The Mighty Must alone
   Shall be!
      W. S. Gilbert.

[225]

A CONCORD LOVE–SONG *

SHALL we meet again, love,
   In the distant When, love,
   When the Now is Then, love,
    And the Present Past?
Shall the mystic Yonder,
On which I ponder,
I sadly wonder,
  With thee be cast?

Ah, the joyless fleeting
Of our primal meeting,
And the fateful greeting
  Of the How and Why!
Ah, the Thingness flying
From the Hereness, sighing
For a love undying
  That fain would die!

Ah, the Ifness sadd'ning,
The Whichness madd'ning,
And the But ungladd'ning,
  That lie behind!
When the signless token
Of love is broken
In the speech unspoken
  Of mind to mind!

* By permission of E. H. Bacon & Co.

But the mind perceiveth
When the spirit grieveth,
And the heart relieveth
  Itself of woe;
And the doubt-mists lifted
From the eyes love-gifted
Are rent and rifted
  In the warmer glow.

In the inner Me, love,
As I turn to thee, love,
I seem to see love,
  No Ego there.
But the Meness dead, love,
The Theeness fled, love,
And born instead, love,
  An Usness rare!

James Jeffrey Roche.

A SONG OF SORROW *

(*A Lullabylet for a Magazinelet*)

WAN from the wild and woful West—
  Sleep, little babe, sleep on!
Mother will sing to—you know the rest—
  Sleep, little babe, sleep on!
Softly the sand steals slowly by,
Cursed be the curlew's chittering cry;
By-a-by, oh, by-a-by!
  Sleep, little babe, sleep on!

* By permission of Harper & Bros.

Rosy and sweet come the hush of night—
  Sleep, little babe, sleep on!
(Twig to the lilt, I have got it all right)
  Sleep, little babe, sleep on!
Dark are the dark and darkling days
Winding the webbed and winsome ways,
Homeward she creeps in dim amaze—
  Sleep, little babe, sleep on!
    (But it waked up, drat it!)
            Charles Battell Loomis.

WATERLOO PLACE

W—UW—Wuw—Wuw—Wuw—Wuw—Wuw—
    W—Waterloo Place? yes you
    T—take the first tut—tut—tut—turning
    that faces you,—
Lul—left,—and then kuk—kuk—kuk—kuk—
    kuk—kuk—keep up, Pall Mall 'till you
See the Wuw—wuw——Wuw——Wuw———
  Zounds, Sir, you'll get there before I can tell
  it you!
            H. Cholmondeley-Pennell.

ALL THE SAME IN THE END

(Epitaph in the Homersfield, Eng., Churchyard)

A S I walked by myself, I talked to myself,
    And thus myself said unto me:
  "Look to thyself, and take care of thyself,
    For nobody cares for thee."

So I turned to myself, and answered myself
In the self-same reverie:
"Look to thyself or not to thyself,
The self-same thing it will be."

Isaac Ross.

A APPEAL FOR ARE TO THE SEXTANT OF THE OLD BRICK MEETINOUSE

(By a gasper)

THE sextant of the meetinouse, which sweeps
    And dusts, or is supposed too! and makes
        fiers,
        And lites the gas and sometimes leaves a
            screw loose,
in which case it smells orful—worse than lampile;
And wrings the Bel and toles it when men dyes
to the grief of survivin pardners, and sweeps pathes;
And for the servases gits $100 per annum,
Which them that thinks deer, let em try it;
Getting up be foar star-lite in all weathers and
Kindlin-fires when the wether it is cold
As zero, and like as not green wood for kindlers;
I wouldn't be hired to do it for no some—
But o sextant! there are 1 kermoddity
Which's more than gold, wich doant cost nothin,
Worth more than anything exsep the Sole of Man.
i mean pewer Are, sextent, i mean pewer are!
O it is plenty out o dores, so plenty it doant no
What on airth to dew with itself, but flys about

Scaterin levs and bloin of men's hatts;
in short, jest 'fre as are" out dores.
But o sextant, in our church its scarce as piety,
scarce as bank bills wen agints beg for mischuns,
Wich some say purty often (taint nothin to me,
Wat I give aint nothin to nobody), but o sextant,
u shut 500 mens wimmen and children,
Speshally the latter, up in a tite place,
Some has bad breths, none aint 2 swete,
some is fevery, some is scrofilus, some has bad teeth,
And some haint none, and some aint over clean;
But every 1 on em breethes in and out and out and
    in,
Say 50 times a minit, or 1 million and a half breths
    an our,
Now how long will a church ful of are last at that
    rate,
I ask you, say 15 minutes, and then wats to be did?
Why then they must brethe it all over agin.
And then agin, and so on, till each has took it down,
At least ten times, and let it up again, and wats more
The same individible don't have the privilege
of brethen his own are, and no one's else;
Each one mus take whatever comes to him.
O sextant, don't you know our lungs is bellusses,
To blo the fier of life, and keep it from
goin out; and how can bellusses blow without wind,
And aint wind *are*? i put it to your conscens.
Are is the same to us as milk to babes,
Or water to fish, or pendlums to clox—
Or roots and airbs unto an injun Doctor,
Or little pils to an omepath,

[230]

Or boys to gurls.   Are is for us to brethe,
Wat signifies who preeches if i cant brethe?
Wats Pol?   Wats Pollus? to sinners who are ded?
Ded for want of breth? why sextant, when we die
Its only coz we cant brethe no more—that's all.
And now, O sextant, let me beg of you
2 let a little are into our church.
(Pewer are is sertin proper for the pews)
And do it weak days and Sundays tew—
It aint much trouble—only make a hole
And the are will come in itself;
(It luvs to come in whare it can git warm:)
And o how it will rouse the people up
And sperrit up the preacher, and stop garbs,
And yawns and figgits as effectooal
As wind on the dry Boans the Profit tells of.

Anonymous.

TECHNICAL WHIMSEYS

THE COSMIC EGG

UPON a rock, yet uncreate,
   Amid a chaos inchoate,
   An uncreated being sate;
Beneath him, rock,
Above him, cloud.
And the cloud was rock,
And the rock was cloud.
The rock then growing soft and warm,
The cloud began to take a form,
A form chaotic, vast and vague,
Which issued in the cosmic egg.
Then the Being uncreate
On the egg did incubate,
And thus became the incubator;
And of the egg did allegate,
And thus became the alligator;
And the incubator was potentate,
But the alligator was potentator.

Anonymous.

[232]

ODE ON THE 450TH ANNIVERSARY CELEBRATION AT ETON

THINK of a number: double it
    (If that does not surpass thy wit);
    Subtract a dozen: add a score:
Divide by twenty: multiply
By twice the cube of $x + y$,
And half again as many more:
Then take the twenty-seventh root
And logarithmic sine to boot,
And if the answer show
Just nine times fifty, make it so.

There's something more than half divine
In fifty multiplied by nine:
And never integer has been
So grand as thirty times fifteen:
The total I could doubtless praise
In many other striking ways:
But this at least is very plain,—
The same will never come again.

Then make an exhibition please
And summon guests from far and wide:
And marry mystic melodies
To odes instinct with proper pride.
Invoke the Founder's mighty name,
And boast of Gray's and Shelley's fame:

For this is very sure: that he
Who misses the latest jubilee
Shall not improbably be vexed
By missing equally the next.

Then let us resolutely strive
This mighty fact to keep alive
That 5 times 9 is 45;
    And furthermore the truth to fix
(In their behoof whose course will run
In June of 1981)
    That 54 is 9 times 6.

                              J. K. Stephen.

NURSERY GARDENING

I LEARN, in Kindergarten, all
    The little things are small.

And how to fix a thing that winds.
She says it rests our minds.

And purple paper weaved with blue
The next thing is to do.

And toolyjoor I always learn
How water will not burn.

And then we string some yellow straw;
I wonder what it's for.

And Teacher makes us muddle clay
One time each single day;

And sing about a kitty-cat;
But never learned me that.

N. M.

THE CHEMIST TO HIS LOVE

I LOVE thee, Mary, and thou lovest me—
   Our mutual flame is like th' affinity
   That doth exist between two simple bodies;
I am Potassium to thine Oxygen.
'Tis little that the holy marriage vow
Shall shortly make us one.   That unity
Is, after all, but metaphysical.
Oh, would that I, my Mary, were an acid,
A living acid; thou an alkali
Endowed with human sense, that, brought together,
We both might coalesce into one salt,
One homogeneous crystal.   Oh! that thou
Wert Carbon, and myself were Hydrogen;
We would unite to form olefiant gas,
Or common coal, or naphtha—would to Heaven
That I were Phosphorus, and thou wert Lime!
And we of Lime composed a Phosphuret.
I'd be content to be Sulphuric Acid,
So thou might be Soda; in that case
We should be Glauber's Salt.   Wert thou Magnesia
Instead, we'd form that's named from Epsom.
Couldst thou Potassia be, I Aqua-fortis,

[235]

Our happy union should that compound form,
Nitrate of Potash—otherwise Saltpetre.
And thus our several natures sweetly blent,
We'd live and love together, until death
Should decompose that fleshly tertium quid,
Leaving our souls to all eternity
Amalgamated. Sweet, thy name is Briggs
And mine is Johnson. Wherefore should not we
Agree to form a Johnsonate of Briggs?
We will! The day, the happy day is nigh,
When Johnson shall with beauteous Briggs com-
 bine.

Punch.

ZOÖLOGY

AH! merry is the Madrepore that sits beside the
 sea;
 The cheery little Coralline hath many charms
 for me;
I love the fine Echinoderms, of azure, green, and
 gray,
That handled roughly fling their arms impulsively
 away;
Then bring me here the microscope and let me see
 the cells
Wherein the little Zoöphite like garden floweret
 dwells.

We'll take the fair Anemone from off its rocky seat,
Since Rondeletius has said when fried 'tis good to
 eat.

[236]

Dyspeptics from Sea-Cucumbers a lesson well may
win,
They blithely take their organs out and put some
fresh ones in.
The Rotifer in whirling round may surely bear the
bell,
With Oceanic Hydrozoids that Huxley knows so
well.

You've heard of the Octopus, 'tis a pleasant thing
to know
He has a ganglion makes him blush, not red, but
white as snow;
And why the strange Cercaria, to go a long way
back,
Wears ever, as some ladies do, a fashionable "sac";
And how the Pawn has parasites that on his head
make holes;
Ask Dr. Cobbold, and he'll say they're just like
tiny soles.

Then study well zoölogy, and add unto your store
The tale of Biogenesis and Protoplasmic lore;
As Paley neatly has observed, when into life they
burst,
The frog and the philosopher are just the same at
first;
But what's the origin of life remains a puzzle still,
Let Tyndall, Haeckel, Bastian, go wrangle as they
will.

Punch.

[237]

A BILLET-DOUX

ACCEPT, dear Miss, this article of mine,
    (For what's indefinite, who can define?)
    My case is singular, my house is rural,
Wilt thou, indeed, consent to make it plural?
Something, I feel, pervades my system through.
I can't describe, yet substantively true,
Thy form so feminine, thy mind reflective,
Where all's possessive good, and nought objective.
I'm positive none can compare with thee
In wit and worth's superlative degree.
First person, then, indicative but prove,
Let thy soft passive voice exclaim, "I love!"
Active, in cheerful mood, no longer neuter,
I'll leave my cares, both present, past, and future.
But ah! what torture must I undergo
Till I obtain that little "Yes" or "No!"
Spare me the negative—to save compunction,
Oh, let my preposition meet conjunction!
What could excite such pleasing recollection,
At hearing thee pronounce this interjection,
"I will be thine! thy joys and griefs to share,
Till Heaven shall please to point a period there!"

Anonymous.

[238]

IMITATIVE HARMONY

THE BELLS

Hear the sledges with the bells—
Silver bells—
What a world of merriment their melody foretells!
How they tinkle, tinkle, tinkle,
In the icy air of night!
While the stars that oversprinkle
All the heavens, seem to twinkle
With a crystalline delight;
Keeping time, time, time,
In a sort of Runic rhyme,
To the tintinnabulation that so musically wells
From the bells, bells, bells, bells,
Bells, bells, bells—
From the jingling and the tinkling of the bells.

Hear the mellow wedding-bells,
Golden bells!
What a world of happiness their harmony foretells!
Through the balmy air of night
How they ring out their delight
From the molten-golden notes!
And all in tune,
What a liquid ditty floats
To the turtle-dove that listens, while she gloats
On the moon!

Oh, from out the sounding cells,
What a gush of euphony voluminously wells!
How it swells!
How it dwells
On the Future! how it tells
Of the rapture that impels
To the swinging and the ringing
Of the bells, bells, bells—
Of the bells, bells, bells, bells,
Bells, bells, bells—
To the rhyming and the chiming of the bells!

Hear the loud alarum bells—
Brazen bells!
What a tale of terror, now, their turbulency tells!
In the startled ear of night
How they scream out their affright!
Too much horrified to speak,
They can only shriek, shriek,
Out of tune,
In a clamorous appealing to the mercy of the
fire,
In a mad expostulation with the deaf and frantic
fire
Leaping higher, higher, higher,
With a desperate desire,
And a resolute endeavour,
Now—now to sit or never,
By the side of the pale-faced moon.
Oh, the bells, bells, bells!
What a tale their terror tells
Of despair!

How they clang, and clash, and roar!
What a horror they outpour
On the bosom of the palpitating air!
Yet the ear, it fully knows,
By the twanging
And the clanging,
How the danger ebbs and flows;
Yet the ear distinctly tells,
In the jangling
And the wrangling,
How the danger sinks and swells,
By the sinking or the swelling in the anger of the
bells—
Of the bells—
Of the bells, bells, bells, bells,
Bells, bells, bells—
In the clamour and the clangour of the bells!

Hear the tolling of the bells—
Iron bells!
What a world of solemn thought their monody
compels!
In the silence of the night
How we shiver with affright
At the melancholy menace of their tone!
For every sound that floats
From the rust within their throats,
Is a groan:
And the people—ah, the people—
They that dwell up in the steeple,
All alone,

[241]

And who, tolling, tolling, tolling,
  In that muffled monotone,
Feel a glory in so rolling
  On the human heart a stone—
They are neither man nor woman—
They are neither brute nor human—
    They are Ghouls!
And their king it is who tolls;
And he rolls, rolls, rolls, rolls,
  A pæan from the bells!
And his merry bosom swells
  With the pæan of the bells!
And he dances and he yells;
Keeping time, time, time,
In a sort of Runic rhyme,
To the pæan of the bells—
    Of the bells;
Keeping time, time, time,
In a sort of Runic rhyme,
  To the throbbing of the bells—
Of the bells, bells, bells,
  To the sobbing of the bells;
Keeping time, time, time,
  As he knells, knells, knells,
In a happy Runic rhyme,
  To the rolling of the bells—
Of the bells, bells, bells—
  To the tolling of the bells,
Of the bells, bells, bells, bells,
    Bells, bells, bells—
To the moaning and the groaning of the bells.
                              Edgar Allan Poe.

[242]

THE CATARACT OF LODORE

H OW does the water
        Come down at Lodore?"
        My little boy asked me
        Thus, once on a time;
And moreover he tasked me
    To tell him in rhyme.
        Anon at the word,
There first came one daughter,
    And then came another,
        To second and third
The request of their brother,
And to hear how the water
        Comes down at Lodore,
        With its rush and its roar,
            As many a time
        They had seen it before.
        So I told them in rhyme,
For of rhymes I had store;
And 'twas in my vocation
        For their recreation
        That so I should sing;
Because I was Laureate
        To them and the King.

From its sources which well
    In the tarn on the fell;

[243]

From its fountains
In the mountains,
Its rills and its gills;
Through moss and through brake,
It runs and it creeps
For a while till it sleeps
In its own little lake.
And thence at departing,
Awakening and starting,
It runs through the reeds,
And away it proceeds,
Through meadow and glade,
In sun and in shade,
And through the wood-shelter,
Among crags in its flurry,
Helter-skelter,
Hurry-skurry,
Here it comes sparkling,
And there it lies darkling;
Now smoking and frothing
Its tumult and wrath in,
Till, in this rapid race
On which it is bent,
It reaches the place
Of its steep descent.

The cataract strong
Then plunges along,
Striking and raging
As if a war waging
Its caverns and rocks among;
Rising and leaping,

Sinking and creeping,
Swelling and sweeping,
Showering and springing,
Flying and flinging,
Writhing and wringing,
Eddying and whisking,
Spouting and frisking,
Turning and twisting
  Around and around
With endless rebound:
  Smiting and fighting,
  A sight to delight in;
Confounding, astounding,
Dizzying and deafening the ear with its sound.

Collecting, projecting,
Receding and speeding,
And shocking and rocking,
And darting and parting,
And threading and spreading,
And whizzing and hissing,
And dripping and skipping,
And hitting and splitting,
And shining and twining,
And rattling and battling,
And shaking and quaking,
And pouring and roaring,
And waving and raving,
And tossing and crossing,
And flowing and going,
And running and stunning,
And foaming and roaming,

And dinning and spinning,
And dropping and hopping,
And working and jerking,
And guggling and struggling,
And heaving and cleaving,
And moaning and groaning;

And glittering and frittering,
And gathering and feathering,
And whitening and brightening,
And quivering and shivering,
And hurrying and skurrying,
And thundering and floundering;

Dividing and gliding and sliding,
And falling and brawling and sprawling,
And driving and riving and striving,
And sprinkling and twinkling and wrinkling,
And sounding and bounding and rounding,
And bubbling and troubling and doubling,
And grumbling and rumbling and tumbling,
And clattering and battering and shattering;

Retreating and beating and meeting and sheeting,
Delaying and straying and playing and spraying,
Advancing and prancing and glancing and dancing,
Recoiling, turmoiling and toiling and boiling,
And gleaming and streaming and steaming and
     beaming,
And rushing and flushing and brushing and gushing,
And flapping and rapping and clapping and
     slapping,

[246]

And curling and whirling and purling and twirling,
And thumping and plumping and bumping and
　　jumping,
And dashing and flashing and splashing and
　　clashing;
And so never ending, but always descending,
Sounds and motions forever and ever are blending,
All at once and all o'er, with a mighty uproar,—
And this way the water comes down at Lodore.
Robert Southey.

WHAT IS A WOMAN LIKE?

A WOMAN is like to—but stay—
　　What a woman is like, who can say?
　　There is no living with or without one.
　Love bites like a fly,
　Now an ear, now an eye,
Buz, buz, always buzzing about one.
　When she's tender and kind
　She is like to my mind,
(And Fanny was so, I remember).
　She's like to—Oh, dear!
　She's as good, very near,
As a ripe, melting peach in September.
　If she laugh, and she chat,
　Play, joke, and all that,
And with smiles and good humor she meet me,
　She's like a rich dish
　Of venison or fish,
That cries from the table, Come eat me!

[247]

But she'll plague you and vex you,
Distract and perplex you;
False-hearted and ranging,
Unsettled and changing,
What then do you think, she is like?
   Like sand?   Like a rock?
   Like a wheel?   Like a clock?
Ay, a clock that is always at strike.
Her head's like the island folks tell on,
Which nothing but monkeys can dwell on;
Her heart's like a lemon—so nice
She carves for each lover a slice;
   In truth she's to me,
   Like the wind, like the sea,
Whose raging will hearken to no man;
   Like a mill, like a pill,
   Like a flail, like a whale,
   Like an ass, like a glass
Whose image is constant to no man;
   Like a shower, like a flower,
   Like a fly, like a pie,
   Like a pea, like a flea,
   Like a thief, like—in brief,
She's like nothing on earth—but a woman!
                  Anonymous.

THE KITCHEN CLOCK

KNITTING is the maid o' the kitchen, Milly,
   Doing nothing sits the chore boy, Billy;
   "Seconds reckoned,
Seconds reckoned;

[248]

Every minute,
Sixty in it.
Milly, Billy,
Billy, Milly,
Tick-tock, tock-tick,
Nick-knock, knock-nick,
Knockety-nick, nickety-knock,"
   Goes the kitchen clock.

Closer to the fire is rosy Milly,
Every whit as close and cozy, Billy;
"Time's a-flying,
Worth your trying;
Pretty Milly—
Kiss her, Billy!
Milly, Billy,
Billy, Milly,
Tick-tock, tock-tick,
Now—now, quick—quick!
Knockety-nick, nickety-knock,"—
   Goes the kitchen clock.

Something's happened, very red is Milly,
Billy boy is looking very silly;
"Pretty misses,
Plenty kisses;
Make it twenty,
Take a plenty.
Billy, Milly,
Milly, Billy,
Right—left, left—right,
That's right, all right,

Knockety-nick, nickety-knock,"—
   Goes the kitchen clock.

Weeks gone, still they're sitting, Milly, Billy;
Oh, the winter winds are wondrous chilly!
"Winter weather,
Close together;
Wouldn't tarry,
Better marry.
Milly, Billy,
Billy, Milly,
Two—one, one—two,
Don't wait, 'twon't do,
Knockety-nick, nickety-knock,"—
   Goes the kitchen clock.

Winters two have gone, and where is Milly?
Spring has come again, and where is Billy?
"Give me credit,
For I did it;
Treat me kindly,
Mind you wind me.
Mister Billy,
Mistress Milly,
My—O, O—my,
By-by, by-by,
Nickety-knock, cradle rock,"—
   Goes the kitchen clock.

John Vance Cheney.

THE FISHERMAN'S CHANT

OH, the fisherman is a happy wight!
   He dibbles by day, and he sniggles by night.
   He trolls for fish, and he trolls his lay—
He sniggles by night, and he dibbles by day.
      Oh, who so merry as he!
      On the river or the sea!
            Sniggling,
            Wriggling
            Eels, and higgling
            Over the price
            Of a nice
            Slice
            Of fish, twice
            As much as it ought to be.

Oh, the fisherman is a happy man!
He dibbles, and sniggles, and fills his can!
With a sharpened hook, and a sharper eye,
He sniggles and dibbles for what comes by.
      Oh, who so merry as he!
      On the river or the sea!
            Dibbling
            Nibbling
            Chub, and quibbling
            Over the price
            Of a nice
            Slice
            Of fish, twice
            As much as it ought to be.
                              F. C. Burnand.

THE RECRUIT

SEZ Corporal Madden to Private McFadden:
    "Bedad, yer a bad un!
    Now turn out yer toes!
  Yer belt is unhookit,
  Yer cap is on crookit,
  Ye may not be dhrunk,
  But, be jabers, ye look it!
    Wan—two!
    Wan—two!
Ye monkey-faced divil, I'll jolly ye through!
    Wan—two!—
    Time! Mark!
Ye march like the aigle in Cintheral Parrk!"

Sez Corporal Madden to Private McFadden:
    "A saint it ud sadden
    To dhrill such a mug!
  Eyes front!—ye baboon, ye!—
  Chin up!—ye gossoon, ye!
  Ye've jaws like a goat—
  Halt! ye leather-lipped loon, ye!
    Wan—two!
    Wan—two!
Ye whiskered orang-outang, I'll fix you!
    Wan—two!—
    Time! Mark!
Ye've eyes like a bat!—can ye see in the dark?"

Sez Corporal Madden to Private McFadden:
    "Yer figger wants padd'n'—
    Sure, man, ye've no shape!
    Behind ye yer shoulders
    Stick out like two boulders;
    Yer shins is as thin
    As a pair of pen-holders!
        Wan—two!
        Wan—two!
Yer belly belongs on yer back, ye Jew!
        Wan—two!—
        Time! Mark!
I'm dhry as a dog—I can't shpake but I bark!"

Sez Corporal Madden to Private McFadden:
    "Me heart it ud gladden
    To blacken your eye.
    Ye're gettin' too bold, ye
    Compel me to scold ye,—
    'Tis halt! that I say,—
    Will ye heed what I told ye?
        Wan—two!
        Wan—two!
Be jabers, I'm dhryer than Brian Boru!
        Wan—two!—
        Time! Mark!
What's wur-ruk for chickens is sport for the lark!"

Sez Corporal Madden to Private McFadden:
    "I'll not stay a gaddin',
    Wid dagoes like you!

I'll travel no farther,
I'm dyin' for—wather;—
Come on, if ye like,—
Can ye loan me a quather?
    Ya-as, you—
    What,—two?
And ye'll pay the potheen? Ye're a daisy! Whurroo!
    You'll do!
    Whist!   Mark!
The Rigiment's flattered to own ye, me spark!"
                        Robert William Chambers.

NO!

NO sun—no moon!
    No morn—no noon—
    No dawn—no dusk—no proper time of
        day—
    No sky—no earthly view—
    No distance looking blue—
No road—no street—no "t'other side the way"—
    No end to any Row—
    No indications where the Crescents go—
    No top to any steeple—
No recognitions of familiar people—
    No courtesies for showing 'em—
    No knowing 'em!
No travelling at all—no locomotion,
No inkling of the way—no notion—
    "No go"—by land or ocean—

No mail—no post—
No news from any foreign coast—
No park—no ring—no afternoon gentility—
No company—no nobility—
No warmth, no cheerfulness, no healthful ease,
No comfortable feel in any member—
No shade, no shine, no butterflies, no bees,
No fruits, no flowers, no leaves, no birds,
November!

Thomas Hood.

LAY OF THE DESERTED INFLUENZAED

DOE, doe!
I shall dever see her bore!
Dever bore our feet shall rove
The beadows as of yore!
Dever bore with byrtle boughs
Her tresses shall I twide—
Dever bore her bellow voice
Bake bellody with bide!
Dever shall we lidger bore,
Abid the flow'rs at dood,
Dever shall we gaze at dight
Upon the tedtder bood!
Ho, doe, doe!
Those berry tibes have flowd,
Ad I shall dever see her bore,
By beautiful! by owd!

[255]

Ho, doe, doe!
I shall dever see her bore,
She will forget be id a bonth,
(Bost probably before)—
She will forget the byrtle boughs,
The flow'rs we plucked at dood,
Our beetigs by the tedtder stars,
Our gazigs at the bood.
Ad I shall dever see agaid
The Lily and the Rose;
The dabask cheek! the sdowy brow!
The perfect bouth ad dose!
Ho, doe, doe!
Those berry tibes have flowd—
Ad I shall dever see her bore,
By beautiful! by owd!!

H. Cholmondeley-Pennell.

BELAGCHOLLY DAYS

CHILLY Dovebber with his boadigg blast
Dow cubs add strips the beddow add the
lawd,
Eved October's suddy days are past—
Add Subber's gawd!

I kdow dot what it is to which I cligg
That stirs to sogg add sorrow, yet I trust
That still I sigg, but as the liddets sigg—
Because I bust.

[256]

Add dow, farewell to roses add to birds,
  To larded fields and tigkligg streablets eke;
Farewell to all articulated words
        I faid would speak.

Farewell, by cherished strolliggs od the sward,
  Greed glades add forest shades, farewell to you;
With sorrowing heart I, wretched add forlord,
        Bid you—achew!!!

Anonymous.

AN INVITATION TO THE ZOOLOGICAL GARDENS

(By a Stuttering Lover)

I HAVE found out a gig-gig-gift for my fuf-fuf-
        fair,
  I have found where the rattlesnakes bub-
        bub-breed;
Will you co-co-come, and I'll show you the bub-
    bub-bear,
  And the lions and tit-tit-tigers at fuf-fuf-feed.

I know where the co-co-cockatoo's song
  Makes mum-mum-melody through the sweet vale;
Where the mum-monkeys gig-gig-grin all the day
    long,
  Or gracefully swing by the tit-tit-tit-tail.

[257]

You shall pip-play, dear, some did-did-delicate joke
  With the bub-bub-bear on the tit-tit-top of his
      pip-pip-pip-pole;
But observe, 'tis forbidden to pip-pip-poke
  At the bub-bub-bear with your pip-pip-pink
      pip-pip-pip-pip-parasol!

You shall see the huge elephant pip-pip-play,
  You shall gig-gig-gaze on the stit-stit-stately
      raccoon;
And then, did-did-dear, together we'll stray,
  To the cage of the bub-bub-blue-faced bab-bab-
      boon.

You wished (I r-r-remember it well,
  And I lul-lul-loved you the m-m-more for the
      wish)
To witness the bub-bub-beautiful pip-pip-pel-
  ican swallow the l-l-live little fuf-fuf-fish!

                                        Punch.

LIMERICKS

SHORT MUSICAL HISTORIES

THERE was a composer named Liszt,
  Who from writing could never desiszt;
    He made Polonaises,
    Quite worthy of praises,
And now that he's gone, he is miszt.

Another composer named Haydn,
The field of Sonata would waydn;
  He wrote the "Creation,"
  Which made a sensation.
And this was the work which he daydn.

A modern composer named Brahms,
Caused in music the greatest of quahms,
  His themes so complex
  Every critic would vex,
From symphonies clear up to psahms.

An ancient musician named Gluck
The manner Italian forsuck:
  He fought with Piccini,
  Gave way to Rossini,
You can find all his views in a buck.

Anonymous.

[259]

PREVALENT POETRY

A WANDERING tribe, called the Siouxs,
   Wear moccasins, having no shiouxs,
      They are made of buckskin,
      With the fleshy side in,
   Embroidered with beads of bright hyiouxs

When out on the war-path, the Siouxs
March single file—never by tiouxs—
   And by "blazing" the trees
   Can return at their ease,
And their way through the forests ne'er liouxs.

All new-fashioned boats he eschiouxs,
And uses the birch-bark caniouxs;
   These are handy and light,
   And, inverted at night,
Give shelter from storms and from dyiouxs.

The principal food of the Siouxs
Is Indian maize, which they briouxs
   And hominy make,
   Or mix in a cake,
And eat it with fork, as they chiouxs.

                                   Anonymous.

TOPOGRAPHICAL

AN old couple living in Gloucester
    Had a beautiful girl, but they loucester;
      She fell from a yacht,
      And never the spacht
    Could be found where the cold waves had
      toucester.

An old lady living in Worcester
Had a gift of a handsome young rorcester;
    But the way that it crough,
    As 'twould never get through,
Was more than the lady was uorcester.

At the bar in the old inn at Leicester
Was a beautiful bar-maid named Heicester;
    She gave to each guest
    Only what was the buest,
And they all, with one accord, bleicester
                    Anonymous.

A SERIOUS LOVE SPELL

A YOUNG lady sings in our choir
    Whose hair is the color of phoir,
      But her charm is unique,
      She has such a fair chique,
    It is really a joy to be nhoir.

[261]

Whenever she looks down the aisle
She gives me a beautiful smaisle,
   And of all of her beaux,
   I am certain she sheaux
She likes me the best all the whaisle.

Last Sunday she wore a new sacque,
Low cut at the front and the bacque.
   And a lovely bouquet
   Worn in such a cute wuet
As only few girls have the knacque.

Some day, ere she grows too antique,
In marriage her hand I shall sique;
   If she's not a coquette,
   Which I'd greatly regruette,
She shall share my $6 a wique.
                    Anonymous.

WILHELMJ

OH, King of the fiddle, Wilhelmj,
   If truly you love me just tellmj;
      Just answer my sigh
      By a glance of your eye,
   Be honest, and don't try to sellmj.

With rapture your music did thrillmj;
With pleasure supreme did it fillmj,
   And if I could believe
   That you meant to deceive—
Wilhelmj, I think it would killmj.
                Robert J. Burdette.

SOME SAINTLY CITIES

A SPORTY young man in St. Pierre
    Had a sweetheart and oft went to sierre.
      She was Gladys by name,
      And one time when he came
    Her mother said: "Gladys St. Hierre."

A globe-trotting man from St. Paul
Made a trip to Japan in the faul.
    One thing he found out,
    As he rambled about,
Was that Japanese ladies St. Taul.

A guy asked two jays at St. Louis
What kind of an Indian the Souis.
    They said: "We're no en-
    Cyclopedia, by hen!"
Said the guy: "If you fellows St. Whouis?"

A bright little maid in St. Thomas
Discovered a suit of pajhomas.
    Said the maiden: "Well, well!
    What they are I can't tell;
But I'm sure that these garments St. Mhomas."
                Ferdinand G. Christgau.

BY CAROLYN WELLS

SAID a bad little youngster named Beauchamp:
"Those jelly-tarts how shall I reauchamp?
To my parents I'd go,
But they always say 'No,'
No matter how much I beseauchamp."

* * *

A very polite man named Hawarden
Went out to plant flowers in his gawarden.
If he trod on a slug,
A worm, or a bug,
He said: "My dear friend, I beg pawarden!"

* * *

There was a young fellow named Knollys,
Who was fond of a good game of kbollys;
He jumped and he ran,—
This clever young man,—
And often he took pleasant kstrollys.

* * *

A lady who lived by the Thames
Had a gorgeous collection of ghames.
She had them reset
In a large coronet
And a number of small diadhames.

* * *

A tutor who tooted the flute
Tried to tutor two tooters to toot.

[264]

Said the two to the tutor,
"Is it harder to toot or
To tutor two tooters to toot?"

*   *   *

A canner, exceedingly canny,
One morning remarked to his granny,
"A canner can can
Anything that he can,
But a canner can't can a can, can he?"

*   *   *

There was a young fellow named Tait,
Who dined with his girl at 8. 08;
But I'd hate to relate
What that fellow named **Tait**
And his tête-à-tête ate at 8. 08!

*   *   *

There was a young man of Typhoo
Who wanted to catch the 2. 02,
But his friend said, "Don't hurry
Or worry or flurry,
It's a minute or two to 2. 02."

*   *   *

"There's a train at 4. 04," said Miss Jenny,
"Four tickets I'll take; have you any?"
Said the man at the door,
"Not four for 4. 04,
For four for 4. 04 is too many!"

[265]

There was a nice fellow named Jenner,
Who sang a phenomenal tenor,
    He had little to spend,
    So I often would lend
The tenor a ten or a tenner.

Carolyn Wells.

There once was a Master of Arts
Who was nuts upon cranberry tarts;
    When he'd eaten his fill,
    He was awfully ill,
But he still was a Master of Arts.

Cosmo Monkhouse.

*   *   *

There once were some learned M.D.'s,
Who captured some germs of disease,
    And infected a train,
    Which without causing pain,
Allowed one to catch it with ease.

Oliver Herford.

*   *   *

There was a young lady of Lynn,
Who was deep in original sin;
    When they said, "Do be good,"
    She said, "Would if I could!"
And straightway went at it ag'in.

Anonymous.

I'd rather have fingers than toes;
I'd rather have ears than a nose;
    And as for my hair
    I'm glad it's all there,
I'll be awfully sad when it goes.
              Gelett Burgess.

*   *   *

There was a young fellow named Clyde;
Who was once at a funeral spied.
    When asked who was dead,
    He smilingly said,
"*I* don't know,—*I* just came for the ride!"
              Anonymous.

*   *   *

There was a young lady of Truro,
Who wished a mahogany bureau;
    But her father said, "Dod!
    All the men on Cape Cod
Couldn't buy a mahogany bureau!"
              Anonymous.

*   *   *

There was a young man of Ostend
Who vowed he'd hold out to the end,
    But when halfway over
    From Calais to Dover,
He done what he didn't intend—
              Anonymous.

[267]

There was an Old Man in a tree
Who was horribly bored by a bee;
    When they said, "Does it buzz?"
    He replied, "Yes, it does!
It's a regular brute of a bee."

    Edward Lear.

    *   *   *

There was an Old Man of St. Bees
Who was stung in the arm by a wasp.
    When asked, "Does it hurt?"
    He replied, "No, it doesn't,
But I thought all the while 'twas a hornet."

    W. S. Gilbert.

    *   *   *

There was an old man of the Rhine,
When asked at what hour he would dine,
    Replied, "At eleven,
    Four, six, three and seven,
And eight and a quarter of nine."

    *   *   *

There was a young man of Laconia,
Whose mother-in-law had pneumonia;
    He hoped for the worst,
    And after March first
They buried her 'neath a begonia.

    *   *   *

There was a young man of the cape
Who always wore trousers of crêpe;
    When asked, "Don't they tear?"
    He replied, "Here and there;
But they keep such a beautiful shape."

[268]

There was a young man of Fort Blainey,
Who proposed to a typist named Janey;
    When his friends said, "Oh, dear!
    She's so old and so queer!"
He replied, "But the day was so rainy!"

                      Anonymous.

INDEX OF TITLES

INDEX OF TITLES

Index of Titles

INDEX OF AUTHORS

INDEX OF AUTHORS

Index of Authors

A Satire Anthology

"The cream of rhymed satire from Aristophanes to Oliver Herford. Shows the same intelligence and good taste as her preceding volumes and furnishes more solid entertainment."—N. Y. *Globe*.

"The book contains many good things and there's a heap of amusement in it."
—Chicago *Tribune*.

"The satires of the ages are brought together in delightful companionship."
—Baltimore *Herald*.

"It fills a useful niche in the reference library, the selections have been made with care."—Brooklyn *Eagle*.

"Will prove useful as well as entertaining."—New York *Evening Sun*.

"The excellent balance displayed in the chronological allotment of more than two hundred selections forestalls criticism."—*The World Today*.